# 中华人民共和国
# 2019 年国民经济和社会发展统计公报

STATISTICAL COMMUNIQUÉ OF THE PEOPLE'S REPUBLIC OF CHINA ON THE 2019 NATIONAL ECONOMIC AND SOCIAL DEVELOPMENT

国 家 统 计 局
National Bureau of Statistics of China

2020年2月28日
February 28, 2020

图书在版编目（CIP）数据

中华人民共和国 2019 年国民经济和社会发展统计公报 = Statistical Communiqué of the People's Republic of China on the 2019 National Economic and Social Development : 汉英对照 / 国家统计局编 . -- 北京 : 中国统计出版社 , 2020.3
　ISBN 978-7-5037-9132-1

Ⅰ . ①中… Ⅱ . ①国… Ⅲ . ①国民经济发展—统计资料—公报—中国— 2019 —汉、英②社会发展—统计资料—公报—中国— 2019 —汉、英 Ⅳ . ① F124-66

中国版本图书馆 CIP 数据核字 (2020) 第 026063 号

## 中华人民共和国 2019 年国民经济和社会发展统计公报

| | |
|---|---|
| 作　　者 | 国家统计局 |
| 责任编辑 | 郭　栋 |
| 装帧设计 | 黄　晨 |
| 出版发行 | 中国统计出版社 |
| 地　　址 | 北京市丰台区西三环南路甲 6 号　　邮政编码 /100073 |
| 网　　址 | http://www.zgtjcbs.com |
| 电　　话 | （010）63376866　63376907（发行部） |
| 印　　刷 | 北京捷迅佳彩印刷有限公司 |
| 经　　销 | 新华书店 |
| 开　　本 | 880×1230 毫米　1/16 |
| 字　　数 | 92 千字 |
| 印　　张 | 5 |
| 版　　别 | 2020 年 3 月第 1 版 |
| 版　　次 | 2020 年 3 月北京第 1 次印刷 |
| 定　　价 | 38.00 元 |

版权所有。未经许可，本书的任何部分不准以任何方式在世界任何地区以任何文字翻印、拷贝、仿制或转载。
如有印装错误，本社发行部负责调换。

# 目 录

一、综合 .................................................. 2

二、农业 .................................................. 8

三、工业和建筑业 ...................................... 10

四、服务业 .............................................. 12

五、国内贸易 ........................................... 15

六、固定资产投资 ...................................... 16

七、对外经济 ........................................... 19

八、财政金融 ........................................... 22

九、居民收入消费和社会保障 ....................... 24

十、科学技术和教育 ................................... 26

十一、文化旅游、卫生健康和体育 ................. 28

十二、资源、环境和应急管理 ....................... 30

# CONTENTS

I. General Outlook .................................................................. 34

II. Agriculture........................................................................ 42

III. Industry and Construction............................................... 44

IV. Service Sector ................................................................ 47

V. Domestic Trade ................................................................ 51

VI. Investment in Fixed Assets ............................................ 52

VII. Foreign Economic Relations ......................................... 54

VIII. Finance and Financial Intermediation ......................... 59

IX. Households Income and Consumption and Social Security .... 61

X. Science & Technology and Education............................. 64

XI. Culture and Tourism, Public Health and Sports ........... 67

XII. Resources, Environment and Emergency Management........ 69

# 中华人民共和国
# 2019 年国民经济和社会发展统计公报[1]

国家统计局
2020 年 2 月 28 日

2019年，面对国内外风险挑战明显上升的复杂局面，在以习近平同志为核心的党中央坚强领导下，各地区各部门以习近平新时代中国特色社会主义思想为指导，全面贯彻党的十九大和十九届二中、三中、四中全会精神，按照党中央、国务院决策部署，坚持稳中求进工作总基调，坚持新发展理念和推动高质量发展，坚持以供给侧结构性改革为主线，着力深化改革扩大开放，持续打好三大攻坚战，统筹稳增长、促改革、调结构、惠民生、防风险、保稳定，扎实做好稳就业、稳金融、稳外贸、稳外资、稳投资、稳预期工作，经济运行总体平稳，发展水平迈上新台阶，发展质量稳步提升，人民生活福祉持续增进，各项社会事业繁荣发展，生态环境质量总体改善，"十三五"规划主要指标进度符合预期，全面建成小康社会取得新的重大进展。

---

[1] 本公报中数据均为初步统计数。各项统计数据均未包括香港特别行政区、澳门特别行政区和台湾省。部分数据因四舍五入的原因，存在总计与分项合计不等的情况。

## 一、综合

初步核算,全年国内生产总值[2]990865亿元,比上年增长6.1%。其中,第一产业增加值70467亿元,增长3.1%;第二产业增加值386165亿元,增长5.7%;第三产业增加值534233亿元,增长6.9%。第一产业增加值占国内生产总值比重为7.1%,第二产业增加值比重为39.0%,第三产业增加值比重为53.9%。全年最终消费支出对国内生产总值增长的贡献率为57.8%,资本形成总额的贡献率为31.2%,货物和服务净出口的贡献率为11.0%。人均国内生产总值70892元,比上年增长5.7%。国民总收入[3]988458亿元,比上年增长6.2%。全国万元国内生产总值能耗[4]比上年下降2.6%。全员劳动生产率[5]为115009元/人,比上年提高6.2%。

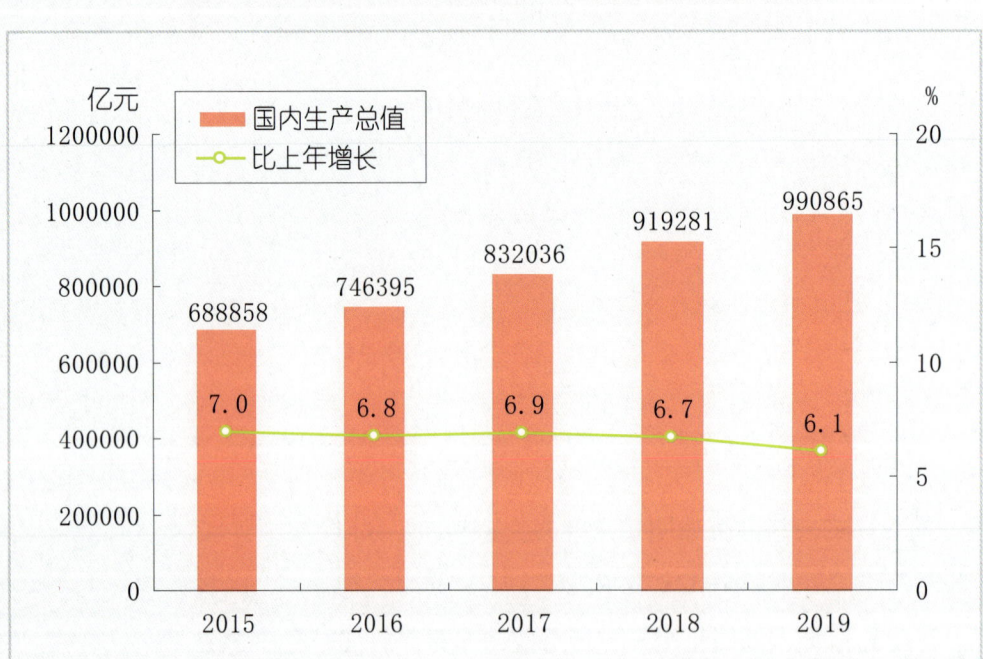

图1 2015-2019年国内生产总值及其增长速度

---

[2]国内生产总值、三次产业及相关行业增加值、地区生产总值、人均国内生产总值和国民总收入绝对数按现价计算,增长速度按不变价格计算。根据第四次全国经济普查结果,对国内生产总值、三次产业及相关行业增加值等相关指标的历史数据进行了修订。

[3]国民总收入,原称国民生产总值,是指一个国家或地区所有常住单位在一定时期内所获得的初次分配收入总额,等于国内生产总值加上来自国外的初次分配收入净额。

[4]万元国内生产总值能耗按2015年价格计算,根据第四次全国经济普查结果对历史数据进行了修订。

[5]全员劳动生产率为国内生产总值(按2015年价格计算)与全部就业人员的比率,根据第四次全国经济普查结果对历史数据进行了修订。

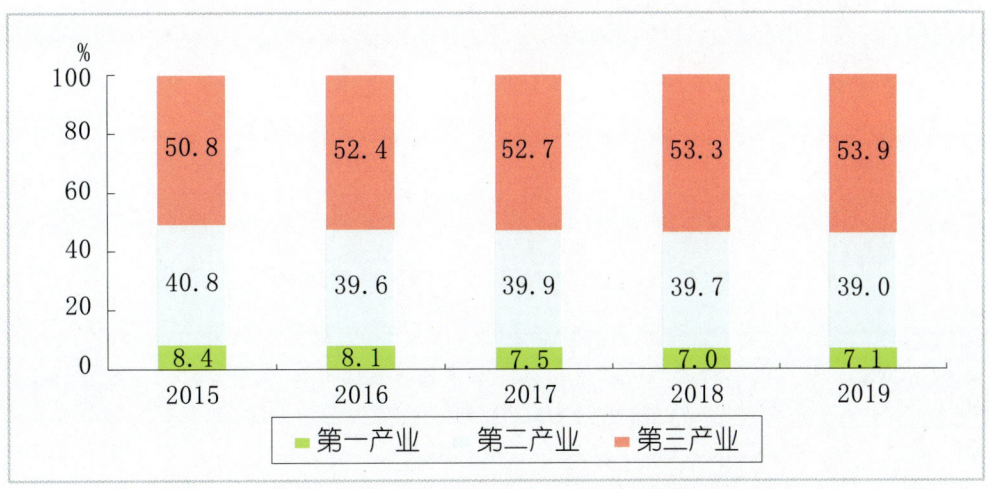

图2　2015-2019年三次产业增加值占国内生产总值比重[6]

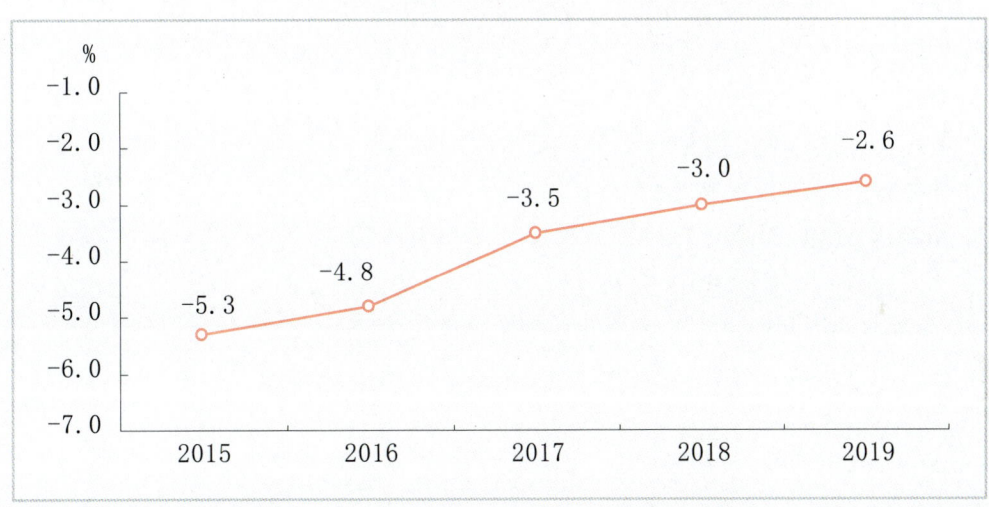

图3　2015-2019年万元国内生产总值能耗降低率[7]

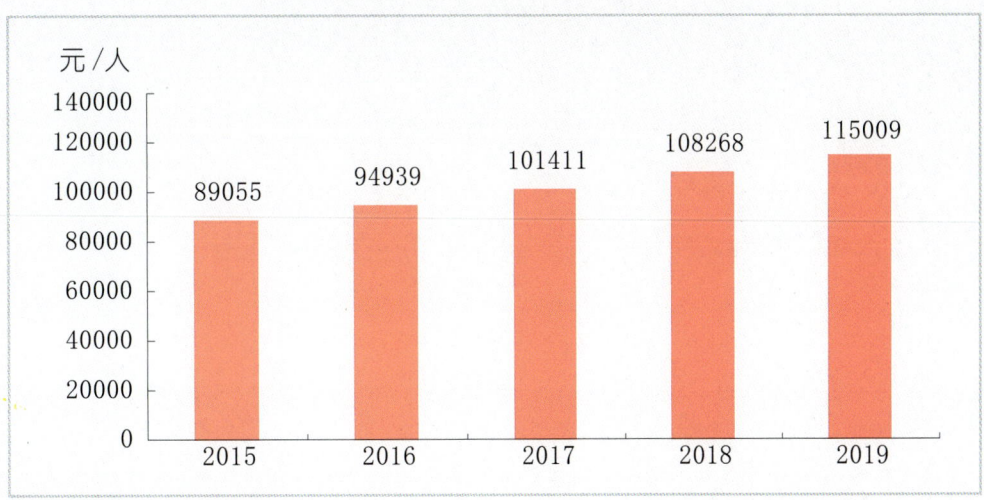

图4　2015-2019年全员劳动生产率[8]

[6] 见注释[2]。
[7] 见注释[4]。
[8] 见注释[5]。

年末全国大陆总人口140005万人,比上年末增加467万人,其中城镇常住人口84843万人,占总人口比重(常住人口城镇化率)为60.60%,比上年末提高1.02个百分点。户籍人口城镇化率为44.38%,比上年末提高1.01个百分点。全年出生人口1465万人,出生率为10.48‰;死亡人口998万人,死亡率为7.14‰;自然增长率为3.34‰。全国人户分离的人口[9]2.80亿人,其中流动人口[10]2.36亿人。

表1　2019年年末人口数及其构成

| 指　　标 | 年末数(万人) | 比重(%) |
|---|---|---|
| 全国总人口 | 140005 | 100.0 |
| 其中:城镇 | 84843 | 60.60 |
| 　　　乡村 | 55162 | 39.40 |
| 其中:男性 | 71527 | 51.1 |
| 　　　女性 | 68478 | 48.9 |
| 其中:0-15岁(含不满16周岁)[11] | 24977 | 17.8 |
| 　　　16-59岁(含不满60周岁) | 89640 | 64.0 |
| 　　　60周岁及以上 | 25388 | 18.1 |
| 　　　其中:65周岁及以上 | 17603 | 12.6 |

图5　2015—2019年常住人口城镇化率

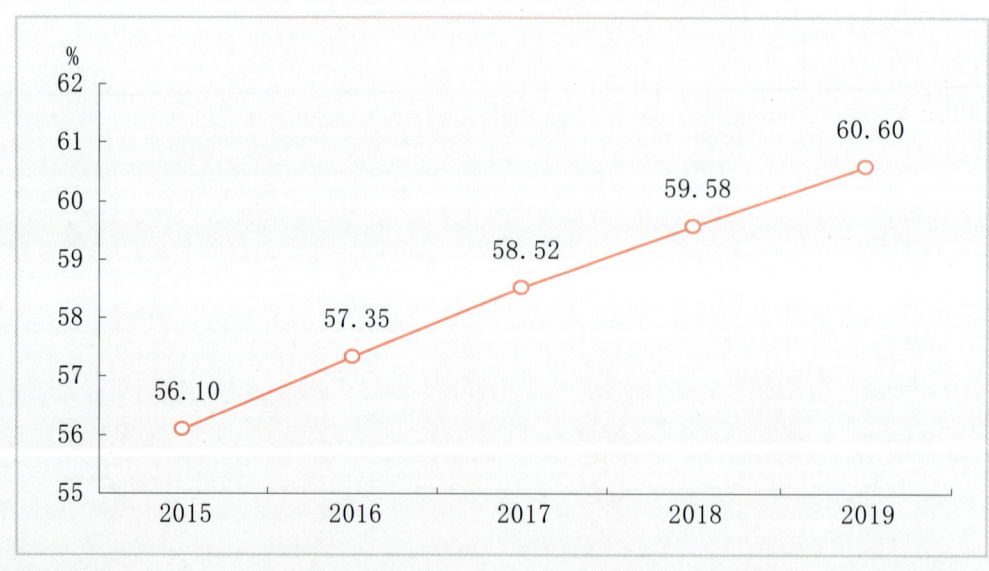

---

[9] 人户分离的人口是指居住地与户口登记地所在的乡镇街道不一致且离开户口登记地半年及以上的人口。

[10] 流动人口是指人户分离人口中扣除市辖区内人户分离的人口。市辖区内人户分离的人口是指一个直辖市或地级市所辖区内和区与区之间,居住地和户口登记地不在同一乡镇街道的人口。

[11] 2019年年末,0-14岁(含不满15周岁)人口为23492万人,15-59岁(含不满60周岁)人口为91125万人。

年末全国就业人员77471万人,其中城镇就业人员44247万人,占全国就业人员比重为57.1%,比上年末上升1.1个百分点。全年城镇新增就业1352万人,比上年少增9万人。年末全国城镇调查失业率为5.2%,城镇登记失业率为3.6%。全国农民工[12]总量29077万人,比上年增长0.8%。其中,外出农民工17425万人,增长0.9%;本地农民工11652万人,增长0.7%。

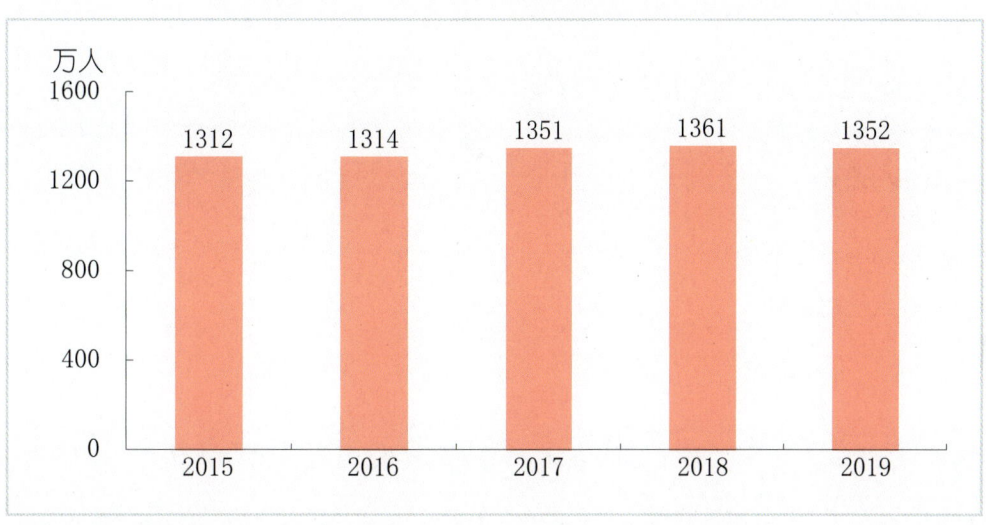

图6　2015-2019年城镇新增就业人数

全年居民消费价格比上年上涨2.9%。工业生产者出厂价格下降0.3%。工业生产者购进价格下降0.7%。固定资产投资价格上涨2.6%。农产品生产者价格[13]上涨14.5%。12月份,70个大中城市新建商品住宅销售价格同比上涨的城市个数为68个,下降的为2个。

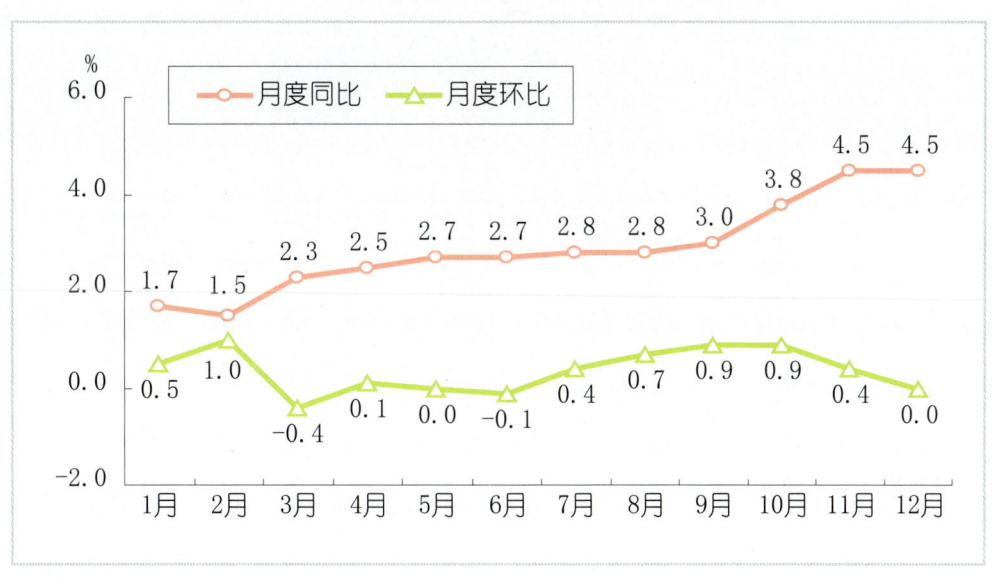

图7　2019年居民消费价格月度涨跌幅度

---

[12]年度农民工数量包括年内在本乡镇以外从业6个月及以上的外出农民工和在本乡镇内从事非农产业6个月及以上的本地农民工。

[13]农产品生产者价格是指农产品生产者直接出售其产品时的价格。

### 表2 2019年居民消费价格比上年涨跌幅度

单位：%

| 指标 | 全国 | 城市 | 农村 |
|---|---|---|---|
| 居民消费价格 | 2.9 | 2.8 | 3.2 |
| 其中：食品烟酒 | 7.0 | 6.7 | 7.9 |
| 衣着 | 1.6 | 1.7 | 1.2 |
| 居住[14] | 1.4 | 1.3 | 1.5 |
| 生活用品及服务 | 0.9 | 0.9 | 0.8 |
| 交通和通信 | -1.7 | -1.8 | -1.4 |
| 教育文化和娱乐 | 2.2 | 2.3 | 1.9 |
| 医疗保健 | 2.4 | 2.5 | 2.1 |
| 其他用品和服务 | 3.4 | 3.5 | 3.1 |

年末国家外汇储备31079亿美元，比上年末增加352亿美元。全年人民币平均汇率为1美元兑6.8985元人民币，比上年贬值4.1%。

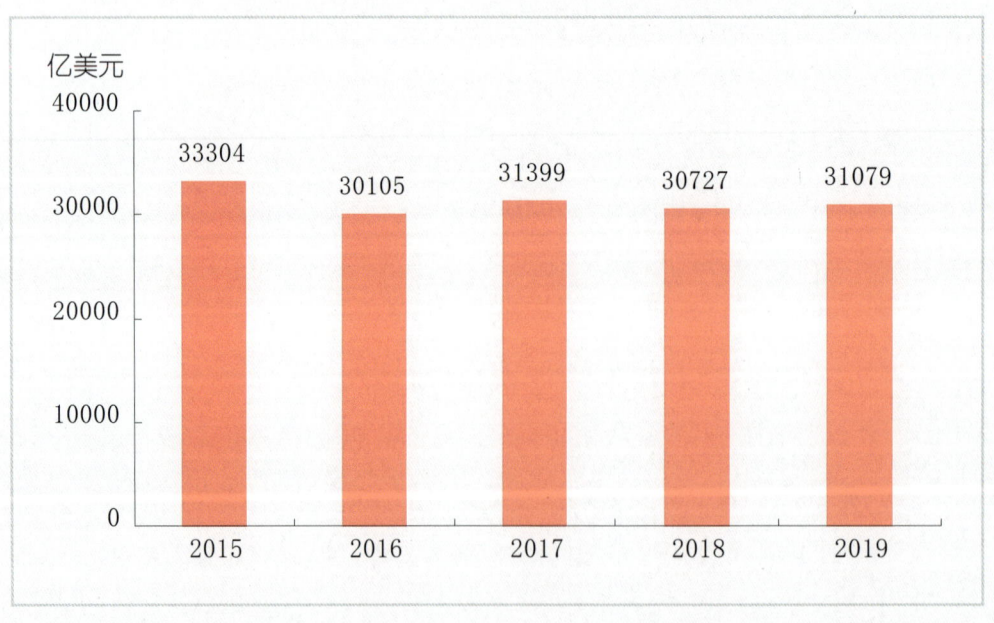

图8 2015-2019年年末国家外汇储备

---

[14]居住类价格包括租赁房房租、住房保养维修及管理、水电燃料等价格。

供给侧结构性改革继续深化。全年全国工业产能利用率[15]为76.6%，比上年提高0.1个百分点。其中，黑色金属冶炼和压延加工业产能利用率为80.0%，提高2.0个百分点；煤炭开采和洗选业产能利用率为70.6%，与上年持平。年末商品房待售面积49821万平方米，比上年末减少2593万平方米。其中，商品住宅待售面积22473万平方米，减少2618万平方米。年末规模以上工业企业资产负债率为56.6%，比上年末下降0.2个百分点[16]。全年教育、生态保护和环境治理业固定资产投资（不含农户）分别比上年增长17.7%和37.2%。"放管服"改革持续深化，微观主体活力不断增强。全年新登记市场主体2377万户，日均新登记企业2万户，年末市场主体总数达1.2亿户。全年减税降费超过2.3万亿元。

新动能保持较快发展。全年规模以上工业中，战略性新兴产业[17]增加值比上年增长8.4%。高技术制造业[18]增加值增长8.8%，占规模以上工业增加值的比重为14.4%。装备制造业[19]增加值增长6.7%，占规模以上工业增加值的比重为32.5%。全年规模以上服务业[20]中，战略性新兴服务业[21]企业营业收入比上年增长12.7%。全年高技术产业投资[22]比上年增长17.3%，工业技术改造投资[23]增长9.8%。全年服务机器人产量346万套，比上年增长38.9%。全年网上零售额[24]106324亿元，按可比口径计算，比上年增长16.5%。

---

[15]产能利用率是指实际产出与生产能力（均以价值量计量）的比率。企业的实际产出是指企业报告期内的工业总产值；企业的生产能力是指报告期内，在劳动力、原材料、燃料、运输等保证供给的情况下，生产设备（机械）保持正常运行，企业可实现并能长期维持的产品产出。

[16]由于统计调查制度规定的口径调整、统计执法、剔除重复数据、企业改革剥离、第四次全国经济普查核实调整等因素，2019年规模以上工业企业财务指标增速及变化按可比口径计算。

[17]工业战略性新兴产业包括新一代信息技术产业，高端装备制造产业，新材料产业，生物产业，新能源汽车产业，新能源产业，节能环保产业和数字创意产业等八大产业中的工业相关行业。2019年工业战略性新兴产业增加值增速按可比口径计算。

[18]高技术制造业包括医药制造业，航空、航天器及设备制造业，电子及通信设备制造业，计算机及办公设备制造业，医疗仪器设备及仪器仪表制造业，信息化学品制造业。

[19]装备制造业包括金属制品业，通用设备制造业，专用设备制造业，汽车制造业，铁路、船舶、航空航天和其他运输设备制造业，电气机械和器材制造业，计算机、通信和其他电子设备制造业，仪器仪表制造业。

[20]规模以上服务业统计范围包括年营业收入1000万元及以上，或年末从业人员50人及以上的交通运输、仓储和邮政业，信息传输、软件和信息技术服务业，房地产业（不含房地产开发经营），租赁和商务服务业，科学研究和技术服务业，水利、环境和公共设施管理业，教育，卫生和社会工作；年营业收入500万元及以上，或年末从业人员50人及以上的居民服务、修理和其他服务业，文化、体育和娱乐业法人单位。

[21]战略性新兴服务业包括新一代信息技术产业，高端装备制造产业，新材料产业，生物产业，新能源汽车产业，新能源产业，节能环保产业和数字创意产业等八大产业中的服务业相关行业，以及新技术与创新创业等相关服务业。2019年战略性新兴服务业企业营业收入增速按可比口径计算。

[22]高技术产业投资包括医药制造、航空航天器及设备制造等六大类高技术制造业投资和信息服务、电子商务服务等九大类高技术服务业投资。

[23]工业技术改造投资是指工业企业利用新技术、新工艺、新设备、新材料对现有设施、工艺条件及生产服务等进行改造提升，实现内涵式发展的投资活动。

[24]网上零售额是指通过公共网络交易平台（主要从事实物商品交易的网上平台，包括自建网站和第三方平台）实现的商品和服务零售额。

区域协调发展扎实推进。分区域看[25]，全年东部地区生产总值511161亿元，比上年增长6.2%；中部地区生产总值218738亿元，增长7.3%；西部地区生产总值205185亿元，增长6.7%；东北地区生产总值50249亿元，增长4.5%。全年京津冀地区生产总值84580亿元，比上年增长6.1%；长江经济带地区生产总值457805亿元，增长6.9%；长江三角洲地区生产总值237253亿元，增长6.4%。

脱贫攻坚成效明显。按照每人每年2300元（2010年不变价）的农村贫困标准计算，年末农村贫困人口551万人，比上年末减少1109万人[26]；贫困发生率[27]0.6%，比上年下降1.1个百分点。全年贫困地区[28]农村居民人均可支配收入11567元，比上年增长11.5%，扣除价格因素，实际增长8.0%。

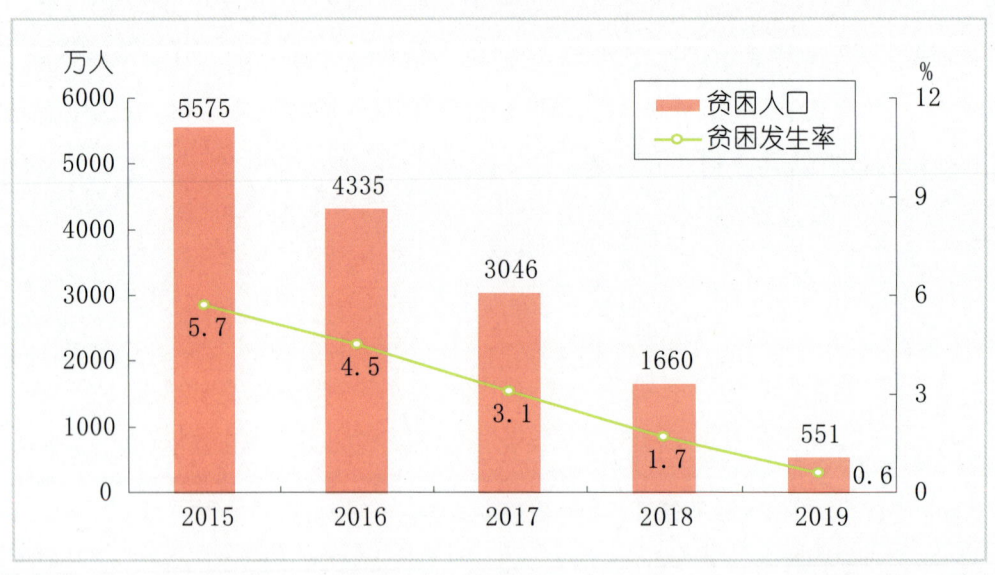

图9　2015-2019年年末全国农村贫困人口和贫困发生率

二、农业

全年粮食种植面积11606万公顷，比上年减少97万公顷。其中，小麦种植面积2373万公顷，减少54万公顷；稻谷种植面积2969万公顷，减少50万公顷；玉米种植面积4128万公顷，减少85万公顷。棉花种植面积334万公顷，减少2万公顷。油料种植面积1293万公顷，增加6万公顷。糖料种植面积162万公顷，减少1万公顷。

---

[25] 东部地区是指北京、天津、河北、上海、江苏、浙江、福建、山东、广东和海南10省（市）；中部地区是指山西、安徽、江西、河南、湖北和湖南6省；西部地区是指内蒙古、广西、重庆、四川、贵州、云南、西藏、陕西、甘肃、青海、宁夏和新疆12省（区、市）；东北地区是指辽宁、吉林和黑龙江3省。
[26] 减贫人口等于当年贫困人口减去上年贫困人口，也相当于当年脱贫人口减去当年返贫人口。
[27] 贫困发生率是指贫困人口占目标调查人口的比重。
[28] 贫困地区包括集中连片特困地区和片区外的国家扶贫开发工作重点县，原共有832个县。2017年开始将新疆阿克苏地区纳入贫困监测范围。

全年粮食产量66384万吨,比上年增加594万吨,增产0.9%。其中,夏粮产量14160万吨,增产2.0%;早稻产量2627万吨,减产8.1%;秋粮产量49597万吨,增产1.1%。全年谷物产量61368万吨,比上年增产0.6%。其中,稻谷产量20961万吨,减产1.2%;小麦产量13359万吨,增产1.6%;玉米产量26077万吨,增产1.4%。

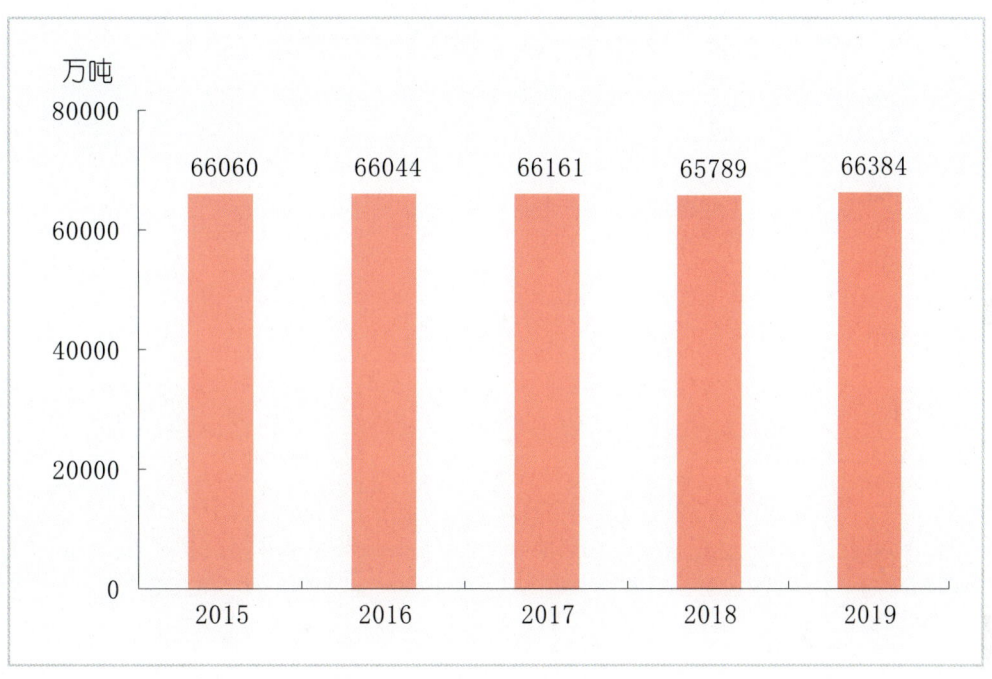

图10　2015–2019年粮食产量

全年棉花产量589万吨,比上年减产3.5%。油料产量3495万吨,增产1.8%。糖料产量12204万吨,增产2.2%。茶叶产量280万吨,增产7.2%。

全年猪牛羊禽肉产量7649万吨,比上年下降10.2%。其中,猪肉产量4255万吨,下降21.3%;牛肉产量667万吨,增长3.6%;羊肉产量488万吨,增长2.6%;禽肉产量2239万吨,增长12.3%。禽蛋产量3309万吨,增长5.8%。牛奶产量3201万吨,增长4.1%。年末生猪存栏31041万头,下降27.5%;生猪出栏54419万头,下降21.6%。

全年水产品产量6450万吨,比上年下降0.1%。其中,养殖水产品产量5050万吨,增长1.0%;捕捞水产品产量1400万吨,下降5.0%。

全年木材产量9028万立方米,比上年增长2.5%。

全年新增耕地灌溉面积27万公顷,新增高效节水灌溉面积146万公顷。

### 三、工业和建筑业

全年全部工业增加值317109亿元，比上年增长5.7%。规模以上工业增加值增长5.7%。在规模以上工业中，分经济类型看，国有控股企业增加值增长4.8%；股份制企业增长6.8%，外商及港澳台商投资企业增长2.0%；私营企业增长7.7%。分门类看，采矿业增长5.0%，制造业增长6.0%，电力、热力、燃气及水生产和供应业增长7.0%。

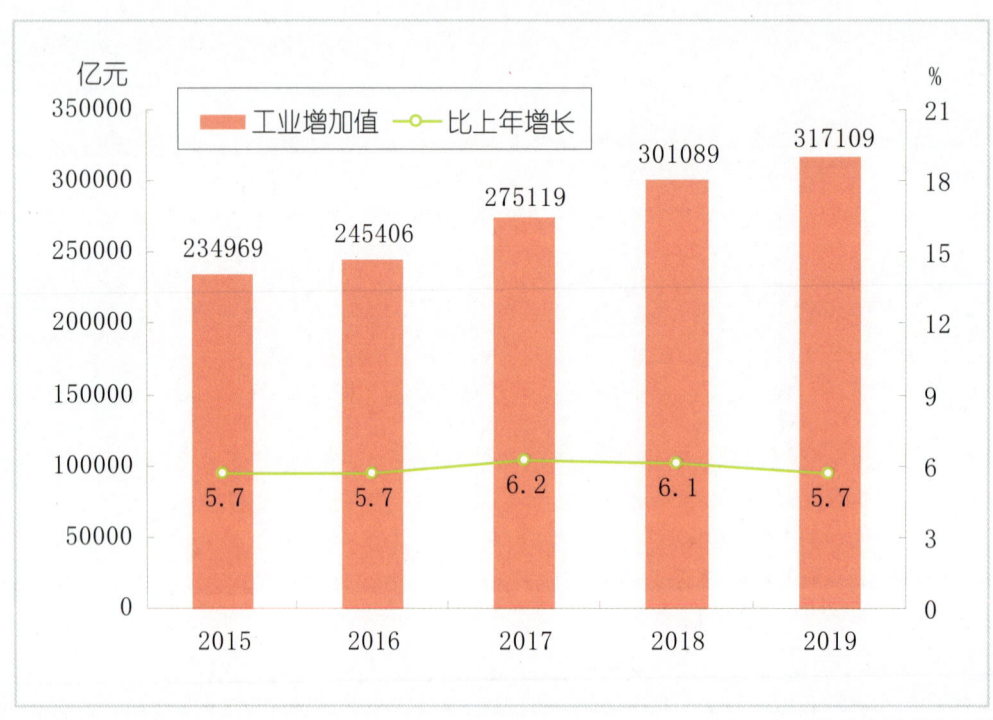

图11　2015-2019年全部工业增加值及其增长速度[29]

全年规模以上工业中，农副食品加工业增加值比上年增长1.9%，纺织业增长1.3%，化学原料和化学制品制造业增长4.7%，非金属矿物制品业增长8.9%，黑色金属冶炼和压延加工业增长9.9%，通用设备制造业增长4.3%，专用设备制造业增长6.9%，汽车制造业增长1.8%，电气机械和器材制造业增长10.7%，计算机、通信和其他电子设备制造业增长9.3%，电力、热力生产和供应业增长6.5%。

---

[29] 见注释[2]。

### 表3  2019年主要工业产品产量及其增长速度[30]

| 产品名称 | 单 位 | 产 量 | 比上年增长（%） |
|---|---|---|---|
| 纱 | 万吨 | 2892.1 | -6.1 |
| 布 | 亿米 | 575.6 | -17.6 |
| 化学纤维 | 万吨 | 5952.8 | 9.9 |
| 成品糖 | 万吨 | 1389.4 | 15.9 |
| 卷烟 | 亿支 | 23642.5 | 1.1 |
| 彩色电视机 | 万台 | 18999.1 | -3.5 |
| 　　其中：液晶电视机 | 万台 | 18689.7 | -1.5 |
| 家用电冰箱 | 万台 | 7904.3 | 6.3 |
| 房间空气调节器 | 万台 | 21866.2 | 4.3 |
| 一次能源生产总量 | 亿吨标准煤 | 39.7 | 5.1 |
| 原煤 | 亿吨 | 38.5 | 4.0 |
| 原油 | 万吨 | 19101.4 | 0.9 |
| 天然气 | 亿立方米 | 1761.7 | 10.0 |
| 发电量 | 亿千瓦小时 | 75034.3 | 4.7 |
| 　　其中：火电[31] | 亿千瓦小时 | 52201.5 | 2.4 |
| 　　　　　水电 | 亿千瓦小时 | 13044.4 | 5.9 |
| 　　　　　核电 | 亿千瓦小时 | 3483.5 | 18.3 |
| 粗钢 | 万吨 | 99634.2 | 7.2 |
| 钢材[32] | 万吨 | 120477.4 | 6.3 |
| 十种有色金属 | 万吨 | 5866.0 | 2.2 |
| 　　其中：精炼铜（电解铜） | 万吨 | 978.4 | 5.5 |
| 　　　　　原　铝（电解铝） | 万吨 | 3504.4 | -2.2 |
| 水泥 | 亿吨 | 23.5 | 4.9 |
| 硫酸（折100%） | 万吨 | 8935.7 | -1.3 |
| 烧碱（折100%） | 万吨 | 3464.4 | -0.3 |
| 乙烯 | 万吨 | 2052.3 | 10.2 |
| 化肥（折100%） | 万吨 | 5731.2 | 6.1 |
| 发电机组（发电设备） | 万千瓦 | 9274.1 | -14.9 |
| 汽车 | 万辆 | 2552.8 | -8.3 |
| 　　其中：基本型乘用车（轿车） | 万辆 | 1018.2 | -16.4 |
| 　　　　　运动型多用途乘用车（SUV） | 万辆 | 876.0 | -3.6 |
| 大中型拖拉机 | 万台 | 27.8 | 5.9 |
| 集成电路 | 亿块 | 2018.2 | 8.9 |
| 程控交换机 | 万线 | 790.5 | -23.7 |
| 移动通信手持机 | 万台 | 170100.6 | -5.5 |
| 微型计算机设备 | 万台 | 34163.2 | 8.2 |
| 工业机器人 | 万台（套） | 17.7 | -3.1 |

[30] 2018年部分产品产量数据根据第四次全国经济普查结果进行了修订，2019年产量增速按可比口径计算。
[31] 火电包括燃煤发电量，燃油发电量，燃气发电量，余热、余压、余气发电量，垃圾焚烧发电量，生物质发电量。
[32] 钢材产量数据中含企业之间重复加工钢材约25200万吨。

年末全国发电装机容量201066万千瓦，比上年末增长5.8%。其中[33]，火电装机容量119055万千瓦，增长4.1%；水电装机容量35640万千瓦，增长1.1%；核电装机容量4874万千瓦，增长9.1%；并网风电装机容量21005万千瓦，增长14.0%；并网太阳能发电装机容量20468万千瓦，增长17.4%。

全年规模以上工业企业利润61996亿元，比上年下降3.3%[34]。分经济类型看，国有控股企业利润16356亿元，比上年下降12.0%；股份制企业45284亿元，下降2.9%，外商及港澳台商投资企业15580亿元，下降3.6%；私营企业18182亿元，增长2.2%。分门类看，采矿业利润5275亿元，比上年增长1.7%；制造业51904亿元，下降5.2%；电力、热力、燃气及水生产和供应业4816亿元，增长15.4%。全年规模以上工业企业每百元营业收入中的成本为84.08元，比上年增加0.18元；营业收入利润率为5.86%，下降0.43个百分点。

全年全社会建筑业增加值70904亿元，比上年增长5.6%。全国具有资质等级的总承包和专业承包建筑业企业利润8381亿元，比上年增长5.1%，其中国有控股企业2585亿元，增长14.5%。

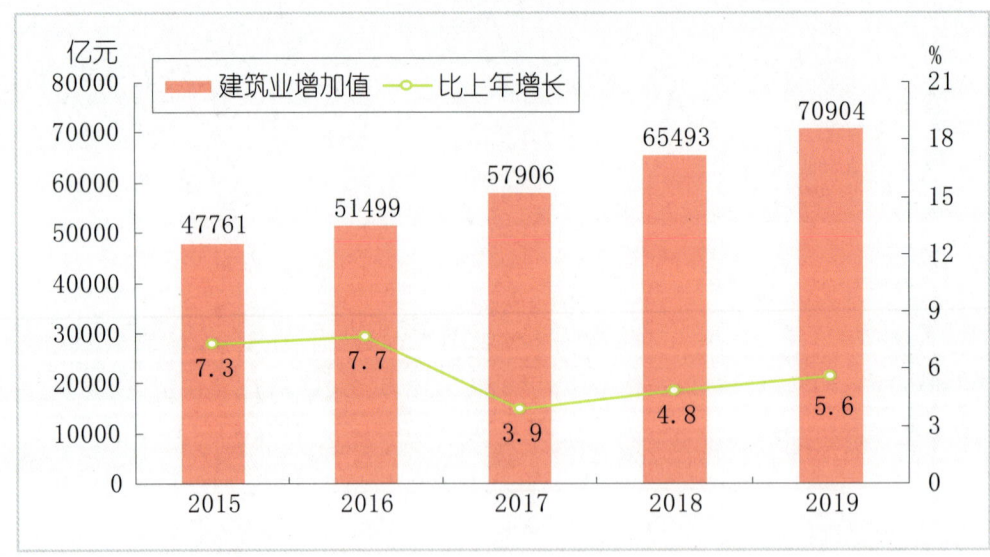

图12　2015–2019年建筑业增加值及其增长速度[35]

### 四、服务业

全年批发和零售业增加值95846亿元，比上年增长5.7%；交通运输、仓储和邮政业增加值42802亿元，增长7.1%；住宿和餐饮业增加值18040亿元，增长6.3%；金融业增加值77077亿元，增长7.2%；房地产业增加值69631亿元，增长3.0%；信息传输、软件和信息技术服务业增加值

---

[33] 少量发电装机容量（如地热等）公报中未列出。
[34] 见注释[16]。
[35] 见注释[2]。

32690亿元，增长18.7%；租赁和商务服务业增加值32933亿元，增长8.7%。全年规模以上服务业企业营业收入比上年增长9.4%，营业利润增长5.4%。

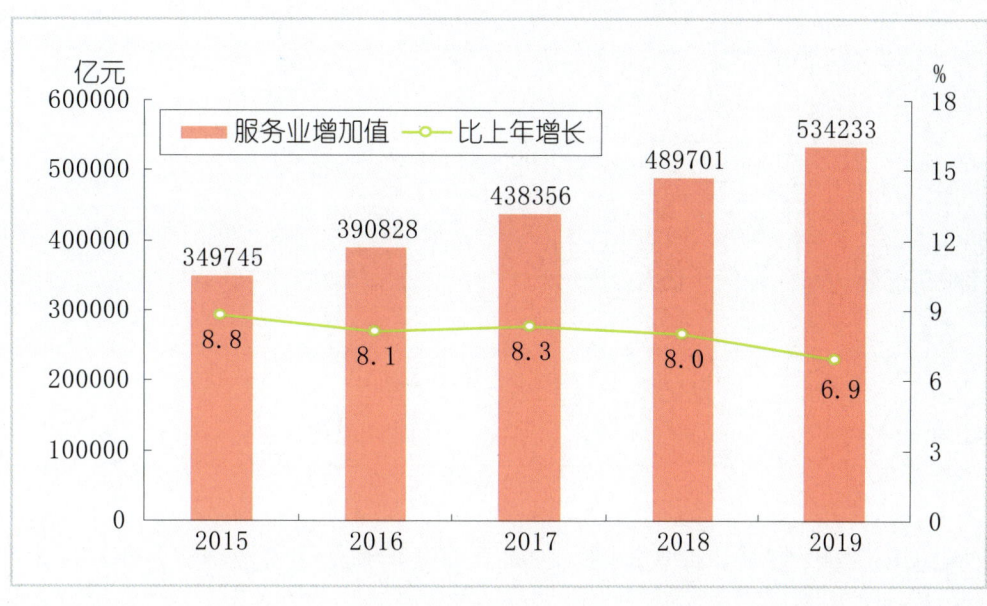

图13　2015-2019年服务业增加值及其增长速度[36]

全年货物运输总量471亿吨，货物运输周转量199290亿吨公里。全年港口[37]完成货物吞吐量140亿吨，比上年增长5.7%，其中外贸货物吞吐量43亿吨，增长4.7%。港口集装箱吞吐量26107万标准箱，增长4.4%。

表4　2019年各种运输方式完成货物运输量及其增长速度[38]

| 指　标 | 单　位 | 绝对数 | 比上年增长（%） |
|---|---|---|---|
| 货物运输总量 | 亿吨 | 470.6 | — |
| 铁　路 | 亿吨 | 43.2 | 7.2 |
| 公　路 | 亿吨 | 343.5 | — |
| 水　运 | 亿吨 | 74.7 | 6.3 |
| 民　航 | 万吨 | 753.2 | 2.0 |
| 管　道 | 亿吨 | 9.1 | 1.8 |
| 货物运输周转量 | 亿吨公里 | 199289.5 | — |
| 铁　路 | 亿吨公里 | 30074.7 | 4.4 |
| 公　路 | 亿吨公里 | 59636.4 | — |
| 水　运 | 亿吨公里 | 103963.0 | 5.0 |
| 民　航 | 亿吨公里 | 263.2 | 0.3 |
| 管　道 | 亿吨公里 | 5352.2 | 1.0 |

[36] 见注释[2]。
[37] 2019年港口统计范围由规模以上港口调整为全国所有港口，相关指标增速按可比口径计算。
[38] 交通运输部根据专项调查，调整2019年公路货物运输量、公路货物运输周转量统计口径，数据与上年不可比。

全年旅客运输总量176亿人次,比上年下降1.9%[39]。旅客运输周转量35349亿人公里,增长3.3%。

**表5  2019年各种运输方式完成旅客运输量及其增长速度**

| 指　标 | 单　位 | 绝对数 | 比上年增长（%） |
|---|---|---|---|
| **旅客运输总量** | 亿人次 | 176.0 | -1.9 |
| 　　铁　路 | 亿人次 | 36.6 | 8.4 |
| 　　公　路 | 亿人次 | 130.1 | -4.8 |
| 　　水　运 | 亿人次 | 2.7 | -2.6 |
| 　　民　航 | 亿人次 | 6.6 | 7.9 |
| **旅客运输周转量** | 亿人公里 | 35349.1 | 3.3 |
| 　　铁　路 | 亿人公里 | 14706.6 | 4.0 |
| 　　公　路 | 亿人公里 | 8857.1 | -4.6 |
| 　　水　运 | 亿人公里 | 80.2 | 0.8 |
| 　　民　航 | 亿人公里 | 11705.1 | 9.3 |

年末全国民用汽车保有量26150万辆（包括三轮汽车和低速货车762万辆），比上年末增加2122万辆，其中私人汽车保有量22635万辆，增加1905万辆。民用轿车保有量14644万辆，增加1193万辆，其中私人轿车保有量13701万辆，增加1112万辆。

全年完成邮政行业业务总量[40]16230亿元，比上年增长31.5%。邮政业全年完成邮政函件业务21.7亿件，包裹业务0.2亿件，快递业务量635.2亿件，快递业务收入7498亿元。全年完成电信业务总量[41]106789亿元，比上年增长62.9%。年末全国电话用户总数179238万户，其中移动电话用户160134万户。移动电话普及率上升至114.4部／百人。固定互联网宽带接入用户[42]44928万户，比上年末增加4190万户，其中固定互联网光纤宽带接入用户[43]41740万户，增加4907万户。全年移动互联网用户接入流量1220亿GB，比上年增长71.6%。全年软件和信息技术服务业[44]完成软件业务收入71768亿元，按可比口径计算，比上年增长15.4%。

---

[39]旅客运输总量包括铁路、公路、水运、民航营业性旅客运输量，其中公路旅客运输量占70%以上。近年来，随着人们出行方式的变化，居民自驾出行、网络约车及拼车人数增长较快，分流了公路客运量，导致旅客运输总量下降。
[40]邮政行业业务总量按2010年价格计算。
[41]电信业务总量按2015年价格计算。
[42]固定互联网宽带接入用户是指报告期末在电信企业登记注册，通过xDSL、FTTx+LAN、FTTH/O以及其他宽带接入方式和普通专线接入公众互联网的用户。
[43]固定互联网光纤宽带接入用户是指报告期末在电信企业登记注册，通过FTTH或FTTO方式接入公众互联网的用户。
[44]软件和信息技术服务业包括软件开发，集成电路设计，信息系统集成和物联网技术服务，运行维护服务，信息处理和存储支持服务，信息技术咨询服务，数字内容服务和其他信息技术服务等行业。

图14　2015-2019年快递业务量及其增长速度

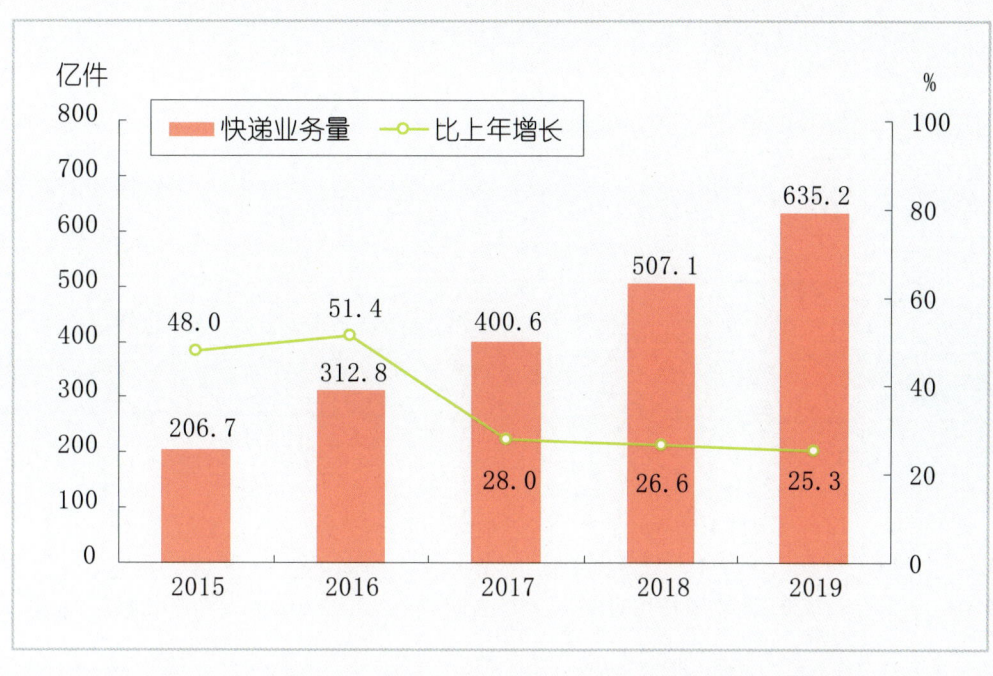

图15　2015-2019年年末固定互联网宽带接入用户数

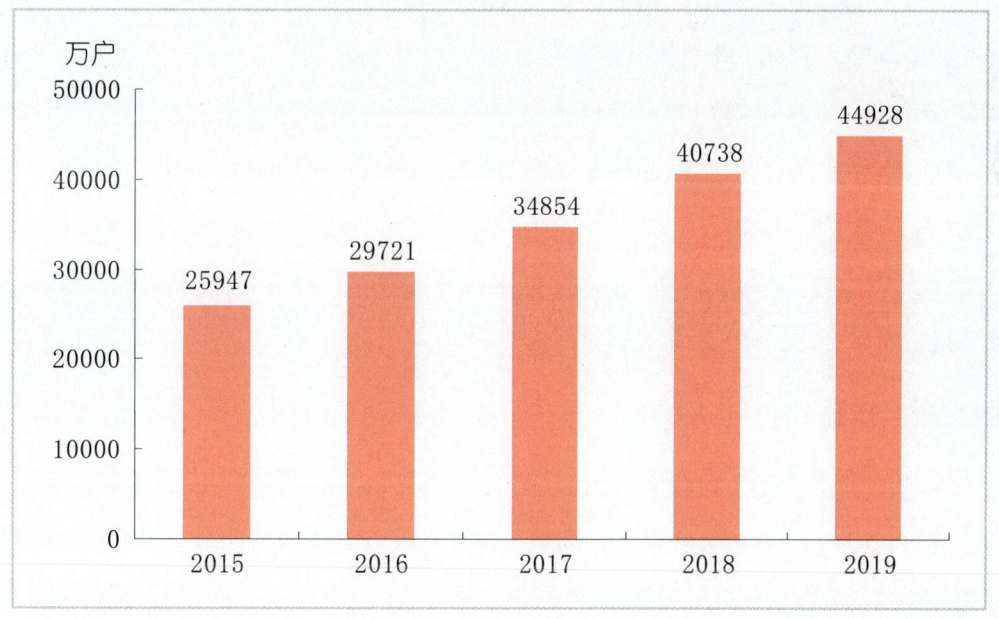

## 五、国内贸易

全年社会消费品零售总额411649亿元，比上年增长8.0%。按经营地统计，城镇消费品零售额351317亿元，增长7.9%；乡村消费品零售额60332亿元，增长9.0%。按消费类型统计，商品零售额364928亿元，增长7.9%；餐饮收入额46721亿元，增长9.4%。

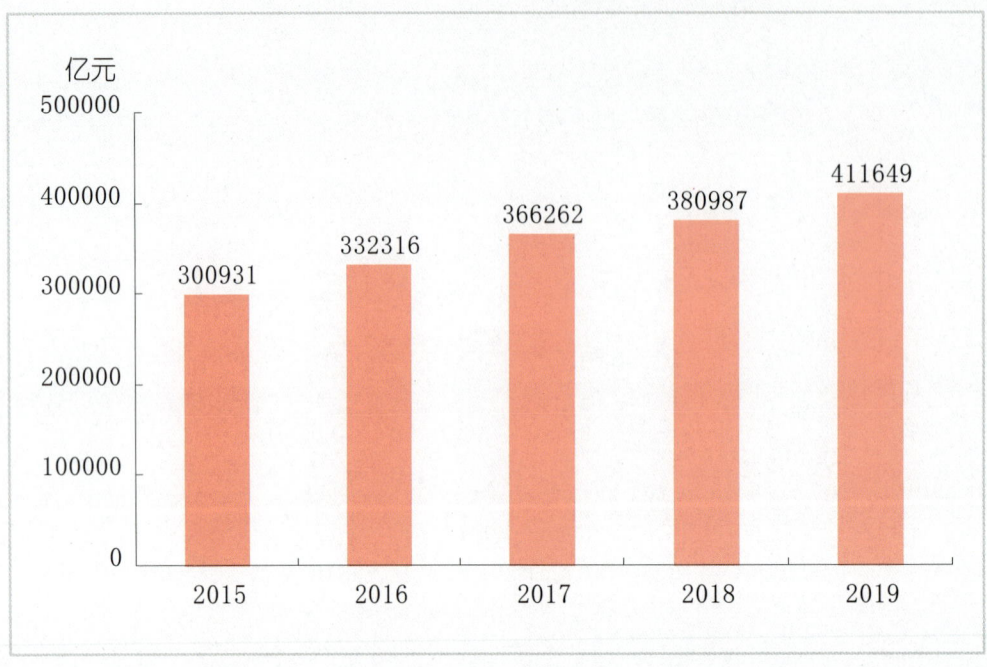

图 16　2015-2019 年社会消费品零售总额

在限额以上单位商品零售额中，粮油、食品类零售额比上年增长 10.2%，饮料类增长 10.4%，烟酒类增长 7.4%，服装、鞋帽、针纺织品类增长 2.9%，化妆品类增长 12.6%，金银珠宝类增长 0.4%，日用品类增长 13.9%，家用电器和音像器材类增长 5.6%，中西药品类增长 9.0%，文化办公用品类增长 3.3%，家具类增长 5.1%，通讯器材类增长 8.5%，建筑及装潢材料类增长 2.8%，石油及制品类增长 1.2%，汽车类下降 0.8%。

全年实物商品网上零售额 85239 亿元，按可比口径计算，比上年增长 19.5%，占社会消费品零售总额的比重为 20.7%，比上年提高 2.3 个百分点。

### 六、固定资产投资

全年全社会固定资产投资[45]560874 亿元，比上年增长 5.1%。其中，固定资产投资（不含农户）551478 亿元，增长 5.4%。分区域看[46]，东部地区投资比上年增长 4.1%，中部地区投资增长 9.5%，西部地区投资增长 5.6%，东北地区投资下降 3.0%。

在固定资产投资（不含农户）中，第一产业投资 12633 亿元，比上年增长 0.6%；第二产业投资 163070 亿元，增长 3.2%；第三产业投资 375775 亿元，增长 6.5%。民间固定资产投资[47]311159

---

[45] 根据第四次全国经济普查、统计执法检查和统计调查制度规定，对2018年固定资产投资数据进行修订，2019年增速按可比口径计算。
[46] 见注释 [25]。
[47] 民间固定资产投资是指具有集体、私营、个人性质的内资企事业单位以及由其控股（包括绝对控股和相对控股）的企业单位建造或购置固定资产的投资。

亿元，增长4.7%。基础设施投资[48]增长3.8%。六大高耗能行业投资增长4.7%。

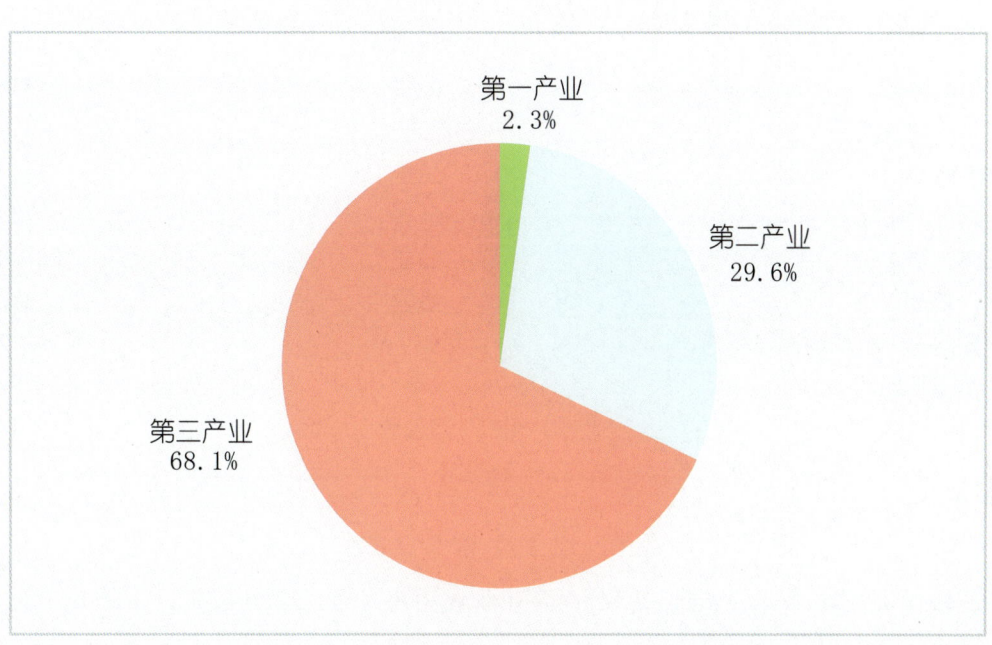

图17　2019年三次产业投资占固定资产投资（不含农户）比重

表6　2019年分行业固定资产投资（不含农户）增长速度

| 行业 | 比上年增长（%） | 行业 | 比上年增长（%） |
| --- | --- | --- | --- |
| 总　计 | 5.4 | 金融业 | 10.4 |
| 农、林、牧、渔业 | 0.7 | 房地产业[49] | 9.1 |
| 采矿业 | 24.1 | 租赁和商务服务业 | 15.8 |
| 制造业 | 3.1 | 科学研究和技术服务业 | 17.9 |
| 电力、热力、燃气及水生产和供应业 | 4.5 | 水利、环境和公共设施管理业 | 2.9 |
| 建筑业 | -19.8 | 居民服务、修理和其他服务业 | -9.1 |
| 批发和零售业 | -15.9 | 教育 | 17.7 |
| 交通运输、仓储和邮政业 | 3.4 | 卫生和社会工作 | 5.3 |
| 住宿和餐饮业 | -1.2 | 文化、体育和娱乐业 | 13.9 |
| 信息传输、软件和信息技术服务业 | 8.6 | 公共管理、社会保障和社会组织 | -15.6 |

---

　　[48]基础设施投资包括交通运输、邮政业，电信、广播电视和卫星传输服务业，互联网和相关服务业，水利、环境和公共设施管理业投资。

　　[49]房地产业投资除房地产开发投资外，还包括建设单位自建房屋以及物业管理、中介服务和其他房地产投资。

### 表7 2019年固定资产投资新增主要生产与运营能力

| 指　标 | 单　位 | 绝对数 |
|---|---|---|
| 新增220千伏及以上变电设备 | 万千伏安 | 23042 |
| 新建铁路投产里程 | 公里 | 8489 |
| 　其中：高速铁路[50] | 公里 | 5474 |
| 增、新建铁路复线投产里程 | 公里 | 6448 |
| 电气化铁路投产里程 | 公里 | 7919 |
| 新改建公路里程 | 公里 | 327626 |
| 　其中：高速公路 | 公里 | 8313 |
| 港口万吨级码头泊位新增通过能力 | 万吨／年 | 12022 |
| 新增民用运输机场 | 个 | 3 |
| 新增光缆线路长度 | 万公里 | 434 |

全年房地产开发投资132194亿元，比上年增长9.9%。其中住宅投资97071亿元，增长13.9%；办公楼投资6163亿元，增长2.8%；商业营业用房投资13226亿元，下降6.7%。

全年全国各类棚户区改造开工316万套，基本建成254万套。全国农村地区建档立卡贫困户危房改造63.8万户[51]。

### 表8 2019年房地产开发和销售主要指标及其增长速度

| 指　标 | 单　位 | 绝对数 | 比上年增长（%） |
|---|---|---|---|
| 投资额 | 亿元 | 132194 | 9.9 |
| 　其中：住宅 | 亿元 | 97071 | 13.9 |
| 房屋施工面积 | 万平方米 | 893821 | 8.7 |
| 　其中：住宅 | 万平方米 | 627673 | 10.1 |
| 房屋新开工面积 | 万平方米 | 227154 | 8.5 |
| 　其中：住宅 | 万平方米 | 167463 | 9.2 |
| 房屋竣工面积 | 万平方米 | 95942 | -2.6 |
| 　其中：住宅 | 万平方米 | 68011 | 3.0 |
| 商品房销售面积 | 万平方米 | 171558 | -0.1 |
| 　其中：住宅 | 万平方米 | 150144 | 1.5 |
| 本年到位资金 | 亿元 | 178609 | 7.6 |
| 　其中：国内贷款 | 亿元 | 25229 | 5.1 |
| 　　　　个人按揭贷款 | 亿元 | 27281 | 15.1 |

[50]高速铁路是指线路最大速度200公里／小时及以上的铁路和200公里／小时以下仅运行动车组列车的铁路。

[51]数据为截至2019年年底全国建档立卡贫困户农村危房改造中央任务开工数。

## 七、对外经济

全年货物进出口总额 315505 亿元，比上年增长 3.4%。其中，出口 172342 亿元，增长 5.0%；进口 143162 亿元，增长 1.6%。货物进出口顺差 29180 亿元，比上年增加 5932 亿元。对"一带一路"[52]沿线国家进出口总额 92690 亿元，比上年增长 10.8%。其中，出口 52585 亿元，增长 13.2%；进口 40105 亿元，增长 7.9%。

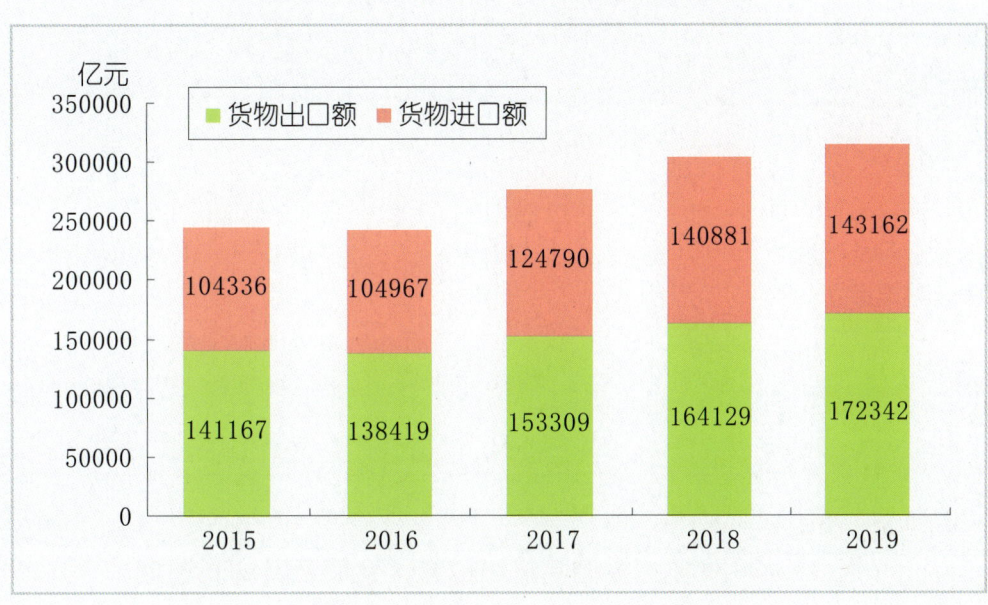

图18　2015-2019年货物进出口总额

表9　2019年货物进出口总额及其增长速度

| 指　　标 | 金额（亿元） | 比上年增长（%） |
| --- | --- | --- |
| 货物进出口总额 | 315505 | 3.4 |
| 　货物出口额 | 172342 | 5.0 |
| 　　其中：一般贸易 | 99546 | 7.8 |
| 　　　　　加工贸易 | 50729 | -3.7 |
| 　　其中：机电产品 | 100631 | 4.4 |
| 　　　　　高新技术产品 | 50427 | 2.1 |
| 　货物进口额 | 143162 | 1.6 |
| 　　其中：一般贸易 | 86599 | 3.1 |
| 　　　　　加工贸易 | 28778 | -7.4 |
| 　　其中：机电产品 | 62596 | -1.8 |
| 　　　　　高新技术产品 | 43978 | -0.8 |
| 货物进出口顺差 | 29180 | — |

[52] "一带一路"是指"丝绸之路经济带"和"21世纪海上丝绸之路"。

### 表10　2019年主要商品出口数量、金额及其增长速度

| 商品名称 | 单 位 | 数　量 | 比上年增长（%） | 金　额（亿元） | 比上年增长（%） |
|---|---|---|---|---|---|
| 钢材 | 万吨 | 6429 | -7.3 | 3699 | -7.1 |
| 纺织纱线、织物及制品 | — | — | — | 8283 | 5.5 |
| 服装及衣着附件 | — | — | — | 10447 | 0.3 |
| 鞋类 | 万吨 | 451 | 0.6 | 3290 | 6.3 |
| 家具及其零件 | — | — | — | 3730 | 5.3 |
| 箱包及类似容器 | 万吨 | 307 | -2.9 | 1878 | 5.1 |
| 玩具 | — | — | — | 2152 | 29.6 |
| 塑料制品 | 万吨 | 1424 | 8.5 | 3333 | 16.2 |
| 集成电路 | 亿个 | 2187 | 0.7 | 7008 | 25.3 |
| 自动数据处理设备及其部件 | 万台 | 148430 | 0.8 | 11415 | 0.5 |
| 手持或车载无线电话机 | 万台 | 99433 | -11.1 | 8611 | -7.8 |
| 集装箱 | 万个 | 242 | -29.0 | 459 | -33.0 |
| 液晶显示板 | 万个 | 150780 | -14.2 | 1475 | -3.4 |
| 汽车 | 万辆 | 122 | 6.1 | 1049 | 8.0 |

### 表11　2019年主要商品进口数量、金额及其增长速度

| 商品名称 | 单 位 | 数　量 | 比上年增长（%） | 金　额（亿元） | 比上年增长（%） |
|---|---|---|---|---|---|
| 谷物及谷物粉 | 万吨 | 1785 | -12.8 | 358 | -7.0 |
| 大豆 | 万吨 | 8851 | 0.5 | 2437 | -2.6 |
| 食用植物油 | 万吨 | 953 | 51.5 | 438 | 39.9 |
| 铁矿砂及其精矿 | 万吨 | 106895 | 0.5 | 6995 | 39.6 |
| 煤及褐煤 | 万吨 | 29967 | 6.3 | 1605 | -1.1 |
| 原油 | 万吨 | 50572 | 9.5 | 16627 | 4.6 |
| 成品油 | 万吨 | 3056 | -8.7 | 1175 | -11.7 |
| 天然气 | 万吨 | 9656 | 6.9 | 2875 | 12.8 |
| 初级形状的塑料 | 万吨 | 3691 | 12.4 | 3670 | -1.3 |
| 纸浆 | 万吨 | 2720 | 9.7 | 1178 | -9.3 |
| 钢材 | 万吨 | 1230 | -6.5 | 973 | -10.2 |
| 未锻轧铜及铜材 | 万吨 | 498 | -6.0 | 2240 | -9.2 |
| 集成电路 | 亿个 | 4451 | 6.6 | 21079 | 2.4 |
| 汽车 | 万辆 | 105 | -7.6 | 3332 | 0.0 |

### 表12  2019年对主要国家和地区货物进出口金额、增长速度及其比重

| 国家和地区 | 出口额（亿元） | 比上年增长（%） | 占全部出口比重（%） | 进口额（亿元） | 比上年增长（%） | 占全部进口比重（%） |
|---|---|---|---|---|---|---|
| 欧盟 | 29564 | 9.6 | 17.2 | 19063 | 5.5 | 13.3 |
| 东盟 | 24797 | 17.8 | 14.4 | 19456 | 9.8 | 13.6 |
| 美国 | 28865 | -8.7 | 16.7 | 8454 | -17.1 | 5.9 |
| 日本 | 9875 | 1.7 | 5.7 | 11837 | -0.6 | 8.3 |
| 中国香港 | 19243 | -3.6 | 11.2 | 626 | 10.9 | 0.4 |
| 韩国 | 7648 | 6.6 | 4.4 | 11960 | -11.4 | 8.4 |
| 中国台湾 | 3799 | 18.3 | 2.2 | 11934 | 1.9 | 8.3 |
| 巴西 | 2453 | 10.8 | 1.4 | 5501 | 7.4 | 3.8 |
| 俄罗斯 | 3434 | 8.5 | 2.0 | 4208 | 7.5 | 2.9 |
| 印度 | 5156 | 2.1 | 3.0 | 1239 | -0.2 | 0.9 |
| 南非 | 1141 | 6.4 | 0.7 | 1784 | -0.8 | 1.2 |

全年服务进出口[53]总额54153亿元，比上年增长2.8%。其中，服务出口19564亿元，增长8.9%；服务进口34589亿元，下降0.4%。服务进出口逆差15025亿元。

全年外商直接投资（不含银行、证券、保险领域）新设立企业40888家，比上年下降32.5%。实际使用外商直接投资金额9415亿元，增长5.8%，折1381亿美元，增长2.4%。其中"一带一路"沿线国家对华直接投资新设立企业5591家，增长24.8%；对华直接投资金额（含通过部分自由港对华投资）576亿元，增长36.0%，折84亿美元，增长30.6%。全年高技术产业实际使用外资2660亿元，增长25.6%，折391亿美元，增长21.7%。

### 表13  2019年外商直接投资（不含银行、证券、保险领域）及其增长速度

| 行业 | 企业数（家） | 比上年增长（%） | 实际使用金额（亿元） | 比上年增长（%） |
|---|---|---|---|---|
| 总计 | 40888 | -32.5 | 9415 | 5.8 |
| 其中：农、林、牧、渔业 | 495 | -33.2 | 38 | -27.9 |
| 制造业 | 5396 | -12.3 | 2416 | -11.0 |
| 电力、热力、燃气及水生产和供应业 | 295 | 3.9 | 239 | -17.6 |
| 交通运输、仓储和邮政业 | 591 | -21.6 | 309 | -1.6 |
| 信息传输、软件和信息技术服务业 | 4295 | -40.5 | 999 | 29.4 |
| 批发和零售业 | 13837 | -39.5 | 614 | -4.5 |
| 房地产业 | 1050 | -0.3 | 1608 | 8.0 |
| 租赁和商务服务业 | 5777 | -36.5 | 1499 | 20.6 |
| 居民服务、修理和其他服务业 | 361 | -25.6 | 37 | -0.4 |

---

[53]服务进出口按照《国际收支手册（第六版）》标准统计，增速按可比口径计算。

全年对外非金融类直接投资额7630亿元，比上年下降4.3%，折1106亿美元，下降8.2%。其中，对"一带一路"沿线国家非金融类直接投资额150亿美元，下降3.8%。

表14　2019年对外非金融类直接投资额及其增长速度

| 行　　业 | 金额（亿美元） | 比上年增长（%） |
| --- | --- | --- |
| 总　计 | 1106.0 | -8.2 |
| 其中：农、林、牧、渔业 | 15.4 | -13.0 |
| 采矿业 | 75.2 | -18.5 |
| 制造业 | 200.8 | 6.7 |
| 电力、热力、燃气及水生产和供应业 | 25.2 | -20.5 |
| 建筑业 | 85.1 | 15.6 |
| 批发和零售业 | 125.7 | 18.6 |
| 交通运输、仓储和邮政业 | 55.5 | -4.3 |
| 信息传输、软件和信息技术服务业 | 61.2 | -10.5 |
| 房地产业 | 48.2 | 22.0 |
| 租赁和商务服务业 | 355.6 | -20.3 |

全年对外承包工程完成营业额11928亿元，比上年增长6.6%，折1729亿美元，增长2.3%。其中，对"一带一路"沿线国家完成营业额980亿美元，增长9.7%，占对外承包工程完成营业额比重为56.7%。对外劳务合作派出各类劳务人员49万人。

**八、财政金融**

全年全国一般公共预算收入190382亿元，比上年增长3.8%。其中税收收入157992亿元，比上年增加1589亿元，增长1.0%。全国一般公共预算支出238874亿元，比上年增长8.1%。

图19　2015-2019年全国一般公共预算收入

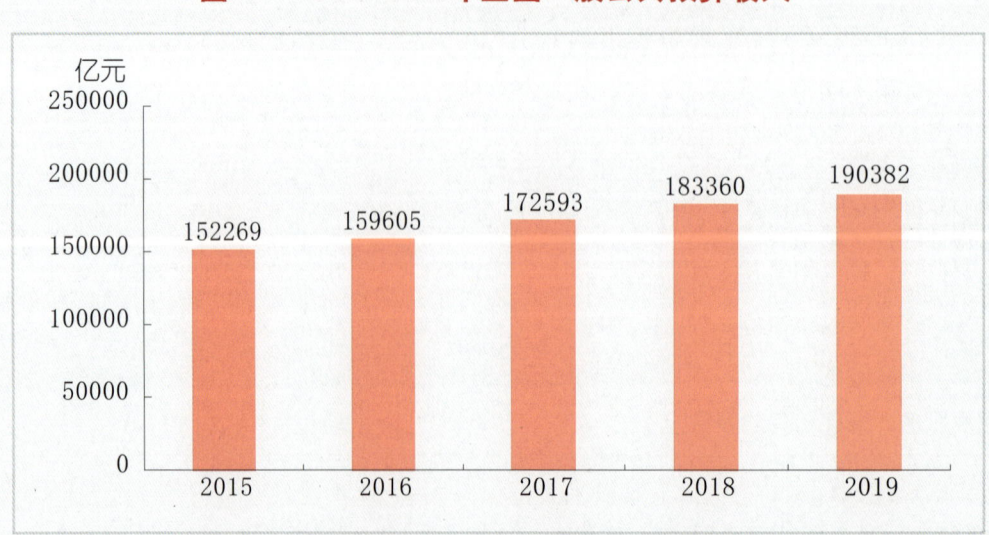

注：图中2015年至2018年数据为全国一般公共预算收入决算数，2019年为执行数。

年末广义货币供应量（M$_2$）余额198.6万亿元，比上年末增长8.7%；狭义货币供应量（M$_1$）余额57.6万亿元，增长4.4%；流通中货币（M$_0$）余额7.7万亿元，增长5.4%。

全年社会融资规模增量[54]25.6万亿元，按可比口径计算，比上年多3.1万亿元；年末社会融资规模存量[55]251.3万亿元，按可比口径计算，比上年末增长10.7%，其中对实体经济发放的人民币贷款余额151.6万亿元，增长12.5%。年末全部金融机构本外币各项存款余额198.2万亿元，比年初增加15.7万亿元，其中人民币各项存款余额192.9万亿元，增加15.4万亿元。全部金融机构本外币各项贷款余额158.6万亿元，增加16.8万亿元，其中人民币各项贷款余额153.1万亿元，增加16.8万亿元。

**表15　2019年年末全部金融机构本外币存贷款余额及其增长速度**

| 指　标 | 年末数（亿元） | 比上年末增长（%） |
| --- | --- | --- |
| 各项存款 | 1981643 | 8.6 |
| 　其中：境内住户存款 | 821296 | 13.4 |
| 　　　其中：人民币 | 813017 | 13.5 |
| 　　　境内非金融企业存款 | 621147 | 5.4 |
| 各项贷款 | 1586021 | 11.9 |
| 　其中：境内短期贷款 | 472380 | 6.6 |
| 　　　境内中长期贷款 | 971805 | 13.7 |

年末主要农村金融机构（农村信用社、农村合作银行、农村商业银行）人民币贷款余额190688亿元，比年初增加20866亿元。全部金融机构人民币消费贷款余额439669亿元，增加61667亿元。其中，个人短期消费贷款余额99226亿元，增加14519亿元；个人中长期消费贷款余额340443亿元，增加47148亿元。

全年沪深交易所A股累计筹资[56]13534亿元，比上年增加2076亿元。首次公开发行A股201只，筹资2490亿元，比上年增加1112亿元，其中科创板股票70只，筹资824亿元；A股再融资（包括公开增发、定向增发、配股、优先股、可转债转股）11044亿元，增加964亿元。全年各类主体通过沪深交易所发行债券（包括公司债、可转债、可交换债、政策性金融债、地方政府债和企业资

---

[54]社会融资规模增量是指一定时期内实体经济从金融体系获得的资金额。2019年，社会融资规模统计口径有所调整。

[55]社会融资规模存量是指一定时期末（月末、季末或年末）实体经济从金融体系获得的资金余额。

[56]沪深交易所股票筹资额按上市日统计，筹资额包括了可转债实际转股金额，2018年、2019年可转债实际转股金额分别为80亿元和995亿元。

产支持证券)筹资71987亿元,比上年增加15109亿元。全国中小企业股份转让系统[57]挂牌公司8953家,全年挂牌公司累计股票筹资265亿元。

全年发行公司信用类债券[58]10.71万亿元,比上年增加2.92万亿元。

全年保险公司原保险保费收入[59]42645亿元,比上年增长12.2%。其中,寿险业务原保险保费收入22754亿元,健康险和意外伤害险业务原保险保费收入8241亿元,财产险业务原保险保费收入11649亿元。支付各类赔款及给付12894亿元。其中,寿险业务给付3743亿元,健康险和意外伤害险业务赔款及给付2649亿元,财产险业务赔款6502亿元。

## 九、居民收入消费和社会保障

全年全国居民人均可支配收入30733元,比上年增长8.9%,扣除价格因素,实际增长5.8%。全国居民人均可支配收入中位数[60]26523元,增长9.0%。按常住地分,城镇居民人均可支配收入42359元,比上年增长7.9%,扣除价格因素,实际增长5.0%。城镇居民人均可支配收入中位数39244元,增长7.8%。农村居民人均可支配收入16021元,比上年增长9.6%,扣除价格因素,实际增长6.2%。农村居民人均可支配收入中位数14389元,增长10.1%。按全国居民五等份收入分组[61],低收入组人均可支配收入7380元,中间偏下收入组人均可支配收入15777元,中间收入组人均可支配收入25035元,中间偏上收入组人均可支配收入39230元,高收入组人均可支配收入76401元。全国农民工人均月收入3962元,比上年增长6.5%。

全年全国居民人均消费支出21559元,比上年增长8.6%,扣除价格因素,实际增长5.5%。其中,人均服务性消费支出[62]9886元,比上年增长12.6%,占居民人均消费支出的比重为45.9%。按常住地分,城镇居民人均消费支出28063元,增长7.5%,扣除价格因素,实际增长4.6%;农村居民人均消费支出13328元,增长9.9%,扣除价格因素,实际增长6.5%。全国居民恩格尔系数为28.2%,比上年下降0.2个百分点,其中城镇为27.6%,农村为30.0%。

---

[57]全国中小企业股份转让系统又称"新三板",是2012年经国务院批准的全国性证券交易场所。全年全国中小企业股份转让系统挂牌公司累计筹资不含优先股,股票筹资按发行报告书的披露日统计。

[58]公司信用类债券包括非金融企业债务融资工具、企业债券以及公司债、可转债等。

[59]原保险保费收入是指保险企业确认的原保险合同保费收入。

[60]人均收入中位数是指将所有调查户按人均收入水平从低到高(或从高到低)顺序排列,处于最中间位置调查户的人均收入。

[61]全国居民五等份收入分组是指将所有调查户按人均收入水平从高到低顺序排列,平均分为五个等份,处于最高20%的收入群体为高收入组,依此类推依次为中间偏上收入组、中间收入组、中间偏下收入组、低收入组。

[62]服务性消费支出是指调查户用于本家庭生活方面的各种非商品性服务费用。

### 图20 2015-2019年全国居民人均可支配收入及其增长速度

### 图21 2019年全国居民人均消费支出及其构成

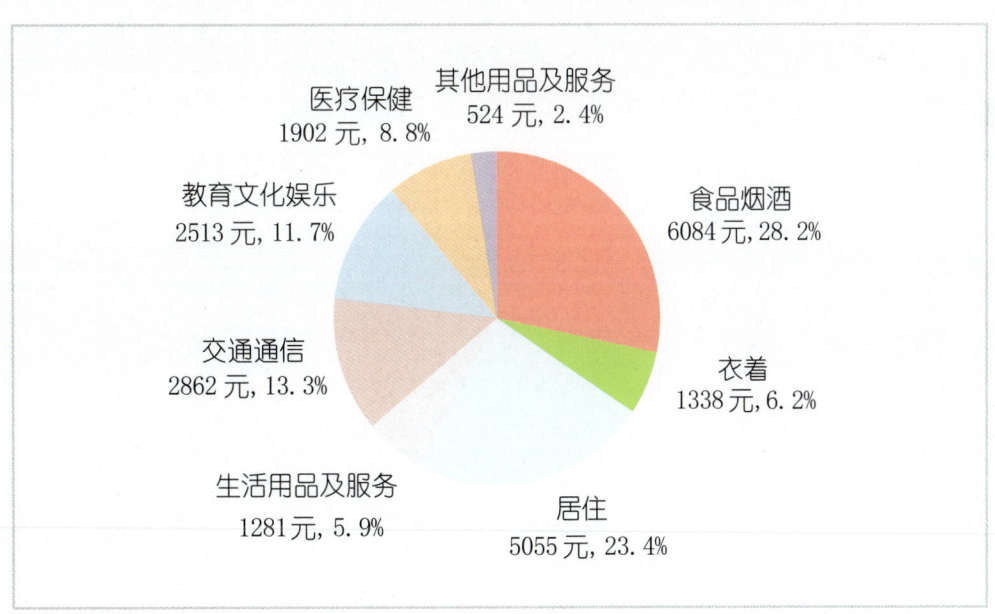

年末全国参加城镇职工基本养老保险人数43482万人，比上年末增加1581万人。参加城乡居民基本养老保险人数53266万人，增加874万人。参加基本医疗保险人数135436万人，增加978万人。其中，参加职工基本医疗保险人数32926万人，增加1245万人；参加城乡居民基本医疗保险人数102510万人。参加失业保险人数20543万人，增加899万人。年末全国领取失业保险金人数228万人。

参加工伤保险人数25474万人，增加1600万人，其中参加工伤保险的农民工8616万人，增加530万人。参加生育保险人数21432万人，增加997万人。年末全国共有861万人享受城市最低生活保障，3456万人享受农村最低生活保障，439万人享受农村特困人员[63]救助供养，全年临时救助[64]918万人次。全年资助7782万人参加基本医疗保险，实施门诊和住院救助6180万人次。全年国家抚恤、补助退役军人和其他优抚对象861万人。

年末全国共有各类提供住宿的社会服务机构3.7万个，其中养老机构3.4万个，儿童服务机构663个。社会服务床位[65]790.1万张，其中养老服务床位761.4万张，儿童服务床位9.7万张。年末共有社区服务中心2.6万个，社区服务站16.7万个。

### 十、科学技术和教育

全年研究与试验发展（R&D）经费支出21737亿元，比上年增长10.5%，与国内生产总值之比为2.19%，其中基础研究经费1209亿元。国家科技重大专项共安排234个课题，国家自然科学基金共资助45192个项目。截至年底，正在运行的国家重点实验室515个，累计建设国家工程研究中心133个，国家工程实验室217个，国家企业技术中心1540家。国家科技成果转化引导基金累计设立21支子基金，资金总规模313亿元。国家级科技企业孵化器[66]1177家，国家备案众创空间[67]1888家。全年境内外专利申请438.0万件，比上年增长1.3%；授予专利权259.2万件，增长5.9%；PCT专利申请受理量[68]为6.1万件。截至年底，有效专利972.2万件，其中境内有效发明专利186.2万件，每万人口发明专利拥有量13.3件。全年商标申请783.7万件，比上年增长6.3%；商标注册640.6万件，增长27.9%。全年共签订技术合同48.4万项，技术合同成交金额22398亿元，比上年增长26.6%。

---

[63] 农村特困人员是指无劳动能力、无生活来源、无法定赡养、抚养、扶养义务人或者其法定义务人无履行义务能力的农村老年人、残疾人以及未满16周岁的未成年人。

[64] 临时救助是国家对遭遇突发事件、意外伤害、重大疾病或其他特殊原因导致基本生活陷入困境，其他社会救助制度暂时无法覆盖或救助之后基本生活暂时仍有严重困难的家庭或个人给予的应急性、过渡性的救助。

[65] 社会服务床位数除收养性机构外，还包括救助类机构、社区类机构的床位。

[66] 国家级科技企业孵化器是指符合《科技企业孵化器管理办法》规定的，以促进科技成果转化、培育科技企业和企业家精神为宗旨，提供物理空间、共享设施和专业化服务的科技创业服务机构，且经过科技部批准认定的科技企业孵化器。

[67] 国家备案众创空间是指符合《发展众创空间工作指引》规定的新型创新创业服务平台，且按照《国家众创空间备案暂行规定》经科技部火炬中心审核备案的众创空间。

[68] PCT专利申请受理量是指国家知识产权局作为PCT专利申请受理局受理的PCT专利申请数量。PCT(Patent Cooperation Treaty)即专利合作条约，是专利领域的一项国际合作条约。

### 图22 2015-2019年研究与试验发展（R&D）经费支出及其增长速度

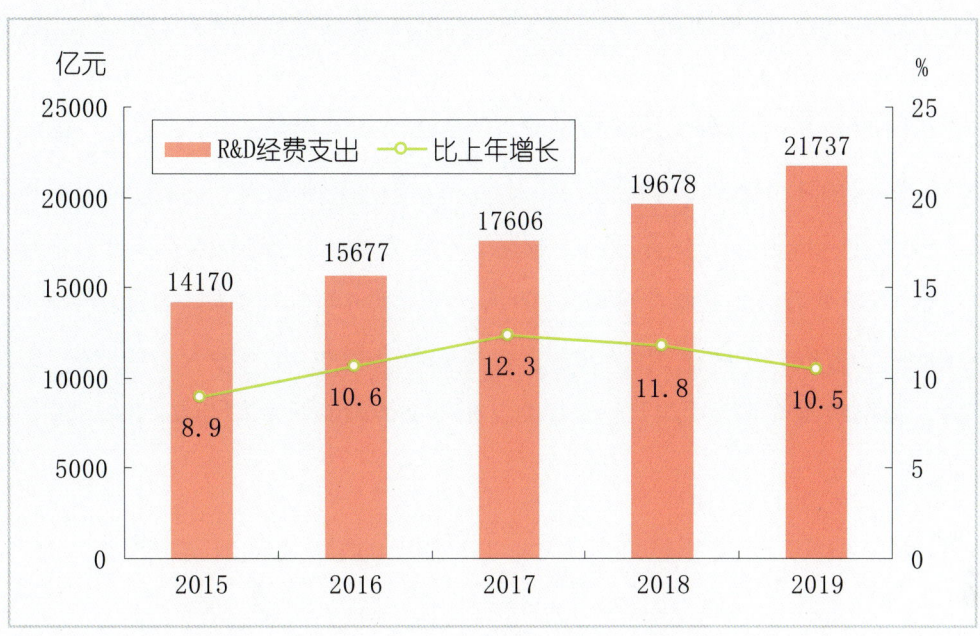

### 表16 2019年专利申请、授权和有效专利情况

| 指　标 | 专利数（万件） | 比上年增长（%） |
|---|---|---|
| **专利申请数** | 438.0 | 1.3 |
| 　其中：境内专利申请 | 417.2 | 1.2 |
| 　其中：发明专利申请 | 140.1 | -9.2 |
| 　　　其中：境内发明专利 | 123.1 | -10.8 |
| **专利授权数** | 259.2 | 5.9 |
| 　其中：境内专利授权 | 245.8 | 6.0 |
| 　其中：发明专利授权 | 45.3 | 4.8 |
| 　　　其中：境内发明专利 | 35.4 | 4.3 |
| **年末有效专利数** | 972.2 | 16.0 |
| 　其中：境内有效专利 | 869.2 | 17.5 |
| 　其中：有效发明专利 | 267.1 | 12.9 |
| 　　　其中：境内有效发明专利 | 186.2 | 16.3 |

全年成功完成32次宇航发射。长征五号遥三运载火箭和高分七号卫星成功发射，长征系列运载火箭发射突破300次大关。嫦娥四号探测器世界上首次实现月球背面软着陆和巡视探测。固体运载火箭海上发射圆满完成。北斗三号全球系统核心星座完成部署，雪龙2号首航南极，首艘国产航母正式列装。

年末全国共有国家质检中心835家。全国现有产品质量、体系和服务认证机构596个，累计完成对72万家企业的认证。全年制定、修订国家标准2021项，其中新制定1448项。全年制造业产品质量合格率[69]为93.86%。

全年研究生教育招生91.7万人，在学研究生286.4万人，毕业生64.0万人。普通本专科招生914.9万人，在校生3031.5万人，毕业生758.5万人。中等职业教育[70]招生600.4万人，在校生1576.5万人，毕业生493.4万人。普通高中招生839.5万人，在校生2414.3万人，毕业生789.2万人。初中招生1638.8万人，在校生4827.1万人，毕业生1454.1万人。普通小学招生1869.0万人，在校生10561.2万人，毕业生1647.9万人。特殊教育招生14.4万人，在校生79.5万人，毕业生9.8万人。学前教育在园幼儿4713.9万人。九年义务教育巩固率为94.8%，高中阶段毛入学率为89.5%。

**图23  2015-2019年普通本专科、中等职业教育及普通高中招生人数**

### 十一、文化旅游、卫生健康和体育

年末全国文化和旅游系统共有艺术表演团体2072个，博物馆3410个。全国共有公共图书馆3189个，总流通[71]87774万人次；文化馆3325个。有线电视实际用户2.12亿户，其中有线数字电视实际用户1.98亿户。年末广播节目综合人口覆盖率为99.1%，电视节目综合人口覆盖率为

---

[69]制造业产品质量合格率是指以产品质量检验为手段，按照规定的方法、程序和标准实施质量抽样检测，判定为质量合格的样品数占全部抽样样品数的百分比，统计调查样本覆盖制造业的29个行业。
[70]中等职业教育包括普通中专、成人中专、职业高中和技工学校。
[71]总流通人次是指本年度内到图书馆场馆接受图书馆服务的总人次，包括借阅书刊、咨询问题以及参加各类读者活动等。

99.4%。全年生产电视剧254部10646集，电视动画片94659分钟。全年生产故事影片850部，科教、纪录、动画和特种影片[72]187部。出版各类报纸315亿份，各类期刊22亿册，图书102亿册（张），人均图书拥有量[73]7.29册（张）。年末全国共有档案馆4136个，已开放各类档案14341万卷（件）。全年全国规模以上文化及相关产业企业营业收入86624亿元，按可比口径计算，比上年增长7.0%。

全年国内游客60.1亿人次，比上年增长8.4%；国内旅游收入57251亿元，增长11.7%。入境游客14531万人次，增长2.9%。其中，外国人3188万人次，增长4.4%；香港、澳门和台湾同胞11342万人次，增长2.5%。在入境游客中，过夜游客6573万人次，增长4.5%。国际旅游收入1313亿美元，增长3.3%。国内居民出境16921万人次，增长4.5%。其中因私出境16211万人次，增长4.6%；赴港澳台出境10237万人次，增长3.2%。

图24  2015-2019年国内游客人次及其增长速度

年末全国共有医疗卫生机构101.4万个，其中医院3.4万个，在医院中有公立医院1.2万个，民营医院2.2万个；基层医疗卫生机构96.0万个，其中乡镇卫生院3.6万个，社区卫生服务中心（站）3.5万个，门诊部（所）26.7万个，村卫生室62.1万个；专业公共卫生机构1.7万个，其中疾病预防控制中心3456个，卫生监督所（中心）3106个。年末卫生技术人员1010万人，其中执业医师和执业助理医师382万人，注册护士443万人。医疗卫生机构床位892万张，其中医院697万张，乡镇卫生院138万张。全年总诊疗人次[74]85.2亿人次，出院人数[75]2.7亿人。

---

[72]特种影片是指采用与常规影院放映在技术、设备、节目方面不同的电影展示方式，如巨幕电影、立体电影、立体特效（4D）电影、动感电影、球幕电影等。

[73]人均图书拥有量是指在一年内全国平均每人能拥有的当年出版图书册数。

[74]总诊疗人次指所有诊疗工作的总人次数，包括门诊、急诊、出诊、预约诊疗、单项健康检查、健康咨询指导（不含健康讲座）人次。

[75]出院人数指报告期内所有住院后出院的人数，包括医嘱离院、医嘱转其他医疗机构、非医嘱离院、死亡及其他人数，不含家庭病床撤床人数。

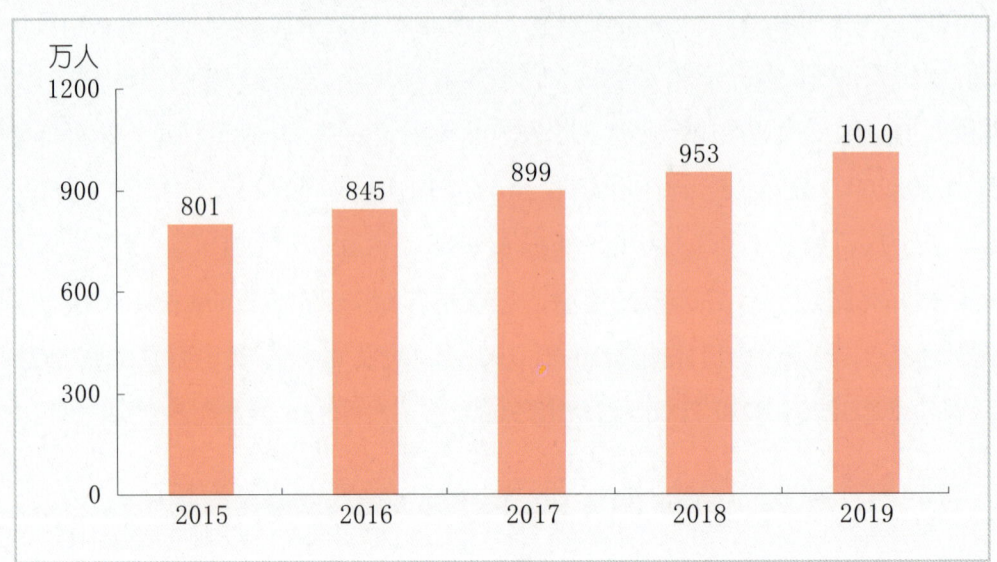

图 25 2015-2019 年年末卫生技术人员人数

全国共有体育场地[76]316.2万个，体育场地面积[77]25.9亿平方米，人均体育场地面积1.86平方米。全年我国运动员在33个运动大项中获得128个世界冠军，共创16项世界纪录。全年我国残疾人运动员在53项国际赛事中获得350个世界冠军。

## 十二、资源、环境和应急管理

全年全国国有建设用地供应总量[78]62.4万公顷，比上年下降3.6%。其中，工矿仓储用地14.7万公顷，增长10.3%；房地产用地[79]14.2万公顷，下降1.4%；基础设施用地33.5万公顷，下降9.5%。

全年水资源总量28670亿立方米。全年总用水量5991亿立方米，比上年下降0.4%。其中，生活用水增长1.9%，工业用水下降2.1%，农业用水下降0.5%，生态补水增长0.5%。万元国内生产总值用水量[80]67立方米，比上年下降6.1%。万元工业增加值用水量42立方米，下降7.2%。人均用水量429立方米，比上年下降0.8%。

全年完成造林面积707万公顷，其中人工造林面积365万公顷，占全部造林面积的51.6%。森林抚育面积773万公顷。截至年底，国家级自然保护区474个。新增水土流失治理面积5.4万平方公里。

初步核算，全年能源消费总量[81]48.6亿吨标准煤，比上年增长3.3%。煤炭消费量增长1.0%，

---

[76]体育场地相关数据来源于第七次全国体育场地普查结果，体育场地普查调查对象不包括军队、铁路系统所属体育场地，数据为截至2018年年底。
[77]体育场地面积指体育训练、比赛、健身场地的有效面积。
[78]国有建设用地供应总量是指报告期内市、县人民政府根据年度土地供应计划依法以出让、划拨、租赁等方式与用地单位或个人签订出让合同或签发划拨决定书、完成交易的国有建设用地总量。
[79]房地产用地是指商服用地和住宅用地的总和。
[80]万元国内生产总值用水量、万元工业增加值用水量按2015年价格计算。
[81]根据第四次全国经济普查结果，对能源消费总量等相关指标历史数据进行了修订。

原油消费量增长6.8%，天然气消费量增长8.6%，电力消费量增长4.5%。煤炭消费量占能源消费总量的57.7%，比上年下降1.5个百分点；天然气、水电、核电、风电等清洁能源消费量占能源消费总量的23.4%，上升1.3个百分点。重点耗能工业企业单位电石综合能耗下降2.1%，单位合成氨综合能耗下降2.4%，吨钢综合能耗下降1.3%，单位电解铝综合能耗下降2.2%，每千瓦时火力发电标准煤耗下降0.3%。全国万元国内生产总值二氧化碳排放下降4.1%。

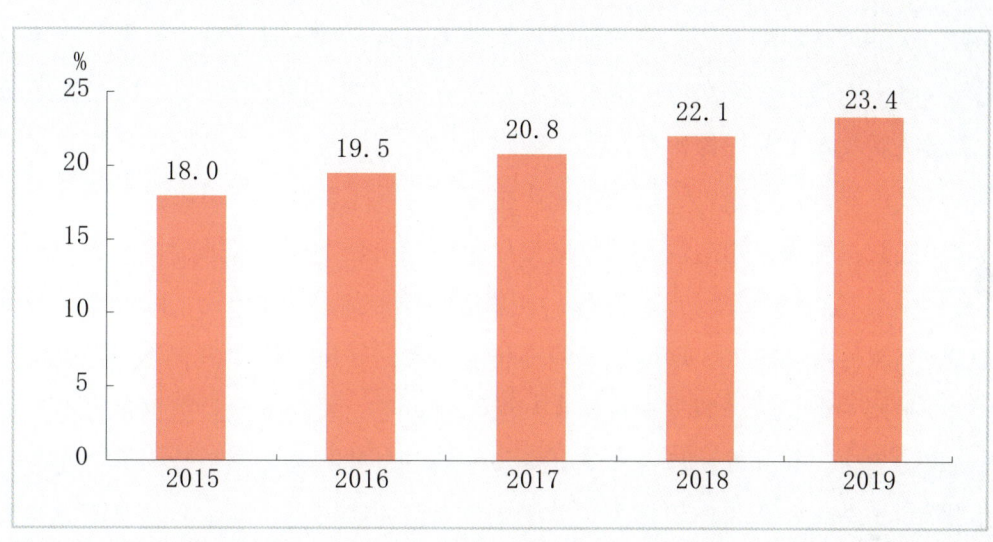

图26　2015–2019年清洁能源消费量占能源消费总量的比重

近岸海域1257个海水水质监测点中，达到国家一、二类海水水质标准的监测点占76.6%，三类海水占7.0%，四类、劣四类海水占16.4%。

在监测的337个地级及以上城市中，空气质量达标的城市占46.6%，未达标的城市占53.4%。细颗粒物（$PM_{2.5}$）未达标城市（基于2015年$PM_{2.5}$年平均浓度未达标的城市）年平均浓度40微克／立方米，比上年下降2.4%。

在开展城市区域声环境监测的322个城市中，声环境质量好的城市占2.5%，较好的占66.8%，一般的占28.9%，较差的占1.9%。

全年平均气温为10.34℃，比上年上升0.25℃。共有5个台风登陆。

全年农作物受灾面积1926万公顷，其中绝收280万公顷。全年因洪涝和地质灾害造成直接经济损失1923亿元，因旱灾造成直接经济损失457亿元，因低温冷冻和雪灾造成直接经济损失28亿元，因海洋灾害造成直接经济损失117亿元。全年大陆地区共发生5.0级以上地震20次，成灾13次，造成直接经济损失约59亿元。全年共发生森林火灾2345起，受灾森林面积1.4万公顷。

全年各类生产安全事故共死亡29519人。工矿商贸企业就业人员10万人生产安全事故死亡人数1.474人，比上年下降4.7%；煤矿百万吨死亡人数0.083人，下降10.8%。道路交通事故万车死亡人数1.80人，下降6.7%。

资料来源：

本公报中户籍人口城镇化率、民用汽车、道路交通事故数据来自公安部；城镇新增就业、登记失业率、社会保障、技工学校数据来自人力资源和社会保障部；外汇储备、汇率数据来自国家外汇管理局；市场主体、质量检验、国家标准制定修订、制造业产品质量合格率数据来自国家市场监督管理总局；减税降费数据来自国家税务总局；水产品产量、新增高效节水灌溉面积数据来自农业农村部；木材产量、造林面积、森林抚育面积、国家级自然保护区数据来自国家林业和草原局；新增耕地灌溉面积、水资源、新增水土流失治理面积数据来自水利部；发电装机容量、新增220千伏及以上变电设备、电力消费量数据来自中国电力企业联合会；港口货物吞吐量、港口集装箱吞吐量、公路运输、水运、新改建公路里程、港口万吨级码头泊位新增通过能力数据来自交通运输部；铁路运输、新建铁路投产里程、增新建铁路复线投产里程、电气化铁路投产里程数据来自中国国家铁路集团有限公司；民航、新增民用运输机场数据来自中国民用航空局；管道数据来自中国石油天然气集团有限公司、中国石油化工集团有限公司、中国海洋石油集团有限公司；邮政业务数据来自国家邮政局；通信业、软件业务收入、新增光缆线路长度等数据来自工业和信息化部；棚户区改造、农村地区建档立卡贫困户危房改造数据来自住房和城乡建设部；货物进出口数据来自海关总署；服务进出口、外商直接投资、对外直接投资、对外承包工程、对外劳务合作等数据来自商务部；财政数据来自财政部；货币金融、公司信用类债券数据来自中国人民银行；境内交易场所筹资数据来自中国证券监督管理委员会；保险业数据来自中国银行保险监督管理委员会；医疗保险、生育保险、资助参加基本医疗保险、实施门诊和住院救助数据来自国家医疗保障局；城乡低保、农村特困人员救助供养、临时救助、社会服务数据来自民政部；优抚对象数据来自退役军人事务部；国家科技重大专项、国家重点实验室、国家科技成果转化引导基金、国家级科技企业孵化器、国家备案众创空间、技术合同等数据来自科学技术部；国家自然科学基金项目数据来自国家自然科学基金委员会；国家工程研究中心、国家工程实验室、国家企业技术中心等数据来自国家发展和改革委员会；专利、商标数据来自国家知识产权局；宇航发射数据来自国家国防科技工业局；教育数据来自教育部；艺术表演团体、博物馆、公共图书馆、文化馆、图书、旅游数据来自文化和旅游部；电视、广播数据来自国家广播电视总局；电影数据来自国家电影局；报纸、期刊数据来自国家新闻出版署；档案数据来自国家档案局；居民出境数据来自国家移民管理局；医疗卫生数据来自国家卫生健康委员会；体育数据来自国家体育总局；残疾人运动员数据来自中国残疾人联合会；国有建设用地供应、海洋灾害造成直接经济损失数据来自自然资源部；万元国内生产总值二氧化碳排放、环境监测等数据来自生态环境部；平均气温、登陆台风数据来自中国气象局；农作物受灾面积、洪涝和地质灾害造成直接经济损失、旱灾造成直接经济损失、低温冷冻和雪灾造成直接经济损失、森林火灾、受灾森林面积、安全生产数据来自应急管理部；地震次数、地震灾害造成直接经济损失数据来自中国地震局；其他数据均来自国家统计局。

# STATISTICAL COMMUNIQUÉ OF THE PEOPLE'S REPUBLIC OF CHINA ON THE 2019 NATIONAL ECONOMIC AND SOCIAL DEVELOPMENT[1]

*National Bureau of Statistics of China*
*February 28, 2020*

In 2019, in the face of mounting risks and challenges both at home and abroad, under the strong leadership of the Central Committee of the Communist Party of China with Comrade Xi Jinping as the core and the guidance of Xi Jinping Thought on Socialism with Chinese Characteristics for a New Era, all regions and departments fully implemented the spirit of the 19th National Congress of the Communist Party of China and the second, third and fourth plenary sessions of the 19th Central Committee of the Communist Party of China, followed the decisions and arrangements made by the CPC Central Committee and the State Council, adhered to the general working guideline of making progress while maintaining stability and the new development philosophy, committed to the high-quality development, focused on the supply-side structural

---

1. All figures in this Communiqué are preliminary statistics. Statistics in this Communiqué do not include Hong Kong SAR, Macao SAR and Taiwan Province. Due to the rounding-off reasons, the subentries may not add up to the aggregate totals.

reform, deepened the reform and opened wider to the world, and unswervingly fought the "Three Critical Battles". All regions and departments took coordinated steps to ensure steady economic growth, advance reform, make structural adjustment, improve living standards, guard against risks and ensure stability, and endeavored to maintain stability in areas of employment, financial sector, foreign trade, foreign investment, domestic investment and market expectation. As a result, the economy was generally stable, the development reached a new stage with steadily raised quality, people's well-being was further enhanced, social undertakings were prospering, and the ecological environment was generally improved. The key indicators of the Thirteenth Five-Year Plan progressed as expected, and major breakthroughs were made in the completion of building a moderately prosperous society in all respects.

## I. General Outlook

According to preliminary estimation, the gross domestic product (GDP)[2] in 2019 was 99,086.5 billion yuan, up by 6.1 percent over the previous year. Of this total, the value added of the primary industry was 7,046.7 billion yuan, up by 3.1 percent, that of the secondary industry was 38,616.5 billion yuan, up by 5.7 percent and that of the tertiary industry was 53,423.3 billion yuan, up by 6.9 percent. The value added of the primary industry accounted for 7.1 percent of the GDP; that of the secondary industry accounted for 39.0 percent; and that of the tertiary industry accounted for 53.9 percent. The contribution of the final consumption expenditure to GDP was 57.8 percent, that of the gross capital formation 31.2 percent and that of the net exports of goods and services 11.0 percent. The per capita GDP in 2019 was 70,892 yuan, up by 5.7 percent compared with the previous year. The gross national income[3] in 2019 was 98,845.8 billion yuan, up by 6.2 percent over the previous year. The national energy consumption per 10,000 yuan worth of GDP[4] went down by 2.6 percent over 2018, and the overall labor productivity[5] reached 115,009 yuan per person in 2019, up by 6.2 percent over the previous year.

---

2. Gross domestic product (GDP), value added of the three and related industries, regional GDP, per capita GDP and gross national income (GNI) as quoted in this Communiqué are calculated at current prices whereas their growth rates are at constant prices. Historical data of GDP, value added of the three and related industries and other related indicators were revised based on the results of the fourth national economic census.

3. Gross national income, also known as gross national product, refers to the total primary distribution of the income created by all the resident units of a country (or a region) during a certain period of time. It equals to gross domestic product plus the net primary distribution of income from abroad.

4. The national energy consumption per 10,000 yuan worth of GDP is calculated at constant prices of 2015. The historical data were revised based on the results of the fourth national economic census.

5. The overall labor productivity refers to the ratio between the GDP (at 2015 constant prices) and the total number of persons employed. The historical data were revised based on the results of the fourth national economic census.

**Figure 1: Gross Domestic Product and Growth Rates 2015-2019**

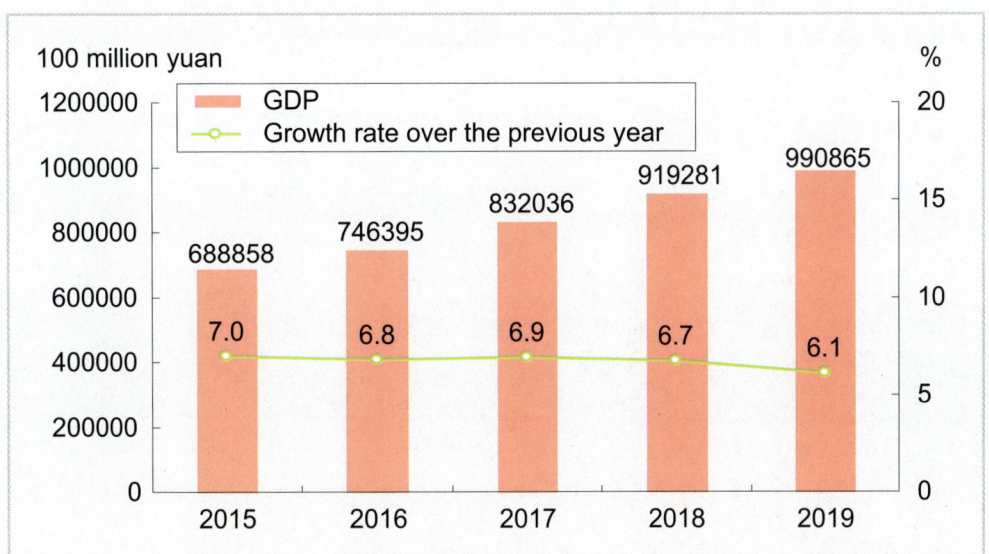

**Figure 2: Shares of the Three Industries' Value Added of GDP 2015-2019**[6]

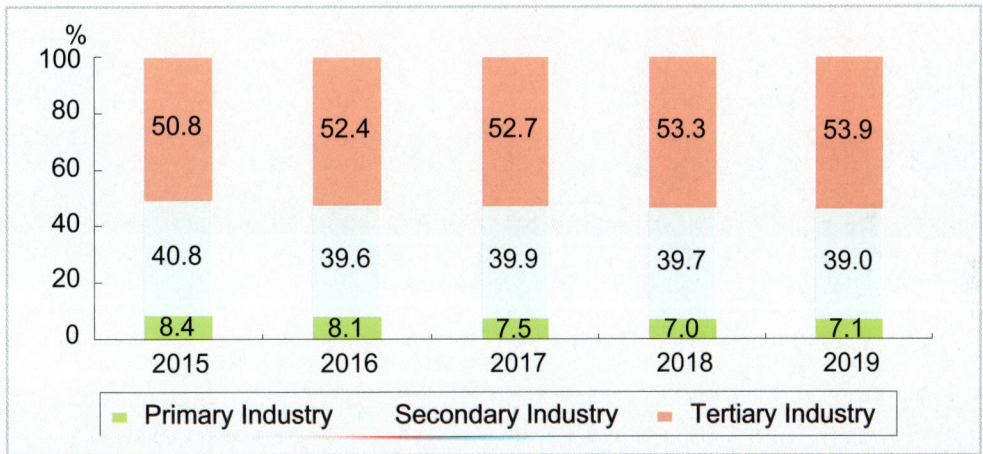

**Figure 3: Changes of Energy Consumption per 10,000 Yuan Worth of GDP 2015-2019**[7]

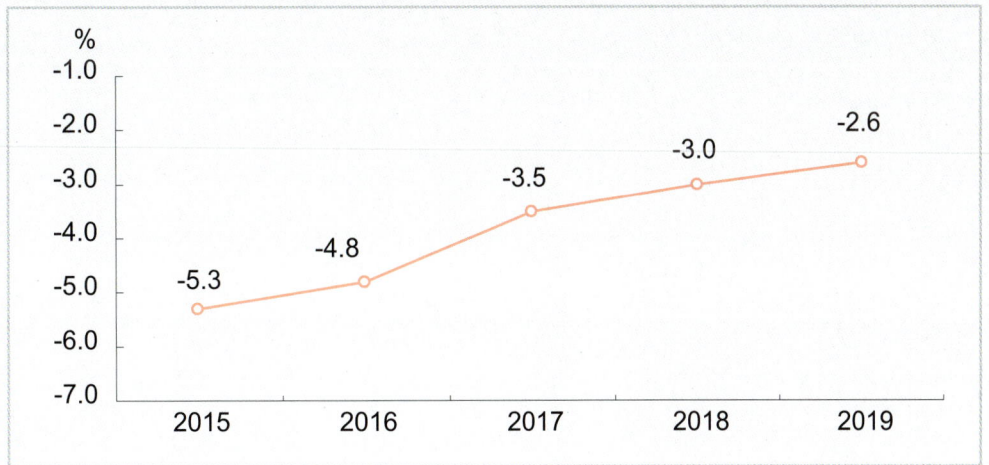

6. See Note 2.
7. See Note 4.

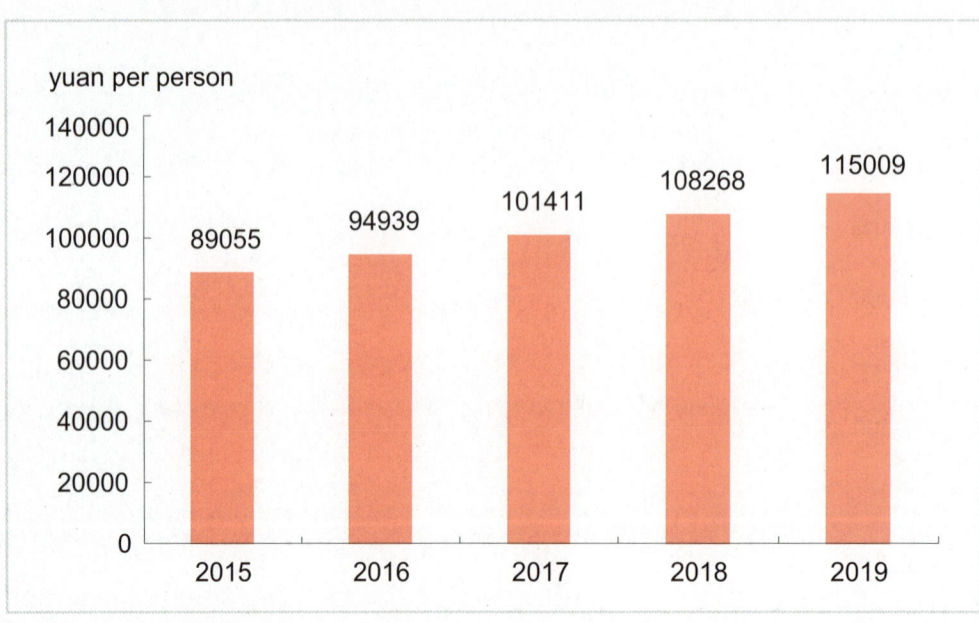

**Figure 4: The Overall Labor Productivity 2015-2019[8]**

By the end of 2019, the total number of Chinese population at the mainland reached 1,400.05 million, an increase of 4.67 million over that at the end of 2018. Of this total, urban permanent residents numbered 848.43 million, accounting for 60.60 percent of the total population (the urbanization rate of permanent residents), 1.02 percentage points higher than that at the end of 2018. The urbanization rate of population with household registration was 44.38 percent, 1.01 percentage points higher than that at the end of 2018. The year 2019 saw 14.65 million births, a crude birth rate of 10.48 per thousand, and 9.98 million deaths, a crude death rate of 7.14 per thousand. The natural growth rate was 3.34 per thousand. The number of population who lived in places other than their household registration areas[9] reached 280 million, of which 236 million were floating population[10].

---

8. See Note 5.
9. Population who live in places other than their household registration areas refers to those who reside in areas other than their household registration and have been away from there for over 6 months.
10. Floating population refers to the population who live in places other than their household registration excluding those with current residences different from the places of their household registration but still in the same city. Population who live in places other than their household registration but still in the same city refers to those whose current residences are different from the registered towns or streets in the same district or in different districts but still in the same municipality or prefecture-level city.

### Table 1: Population and Its Composition by the End of 2019

| Item | Population at Year-end (10,000 persons) | Proportion (%) |
|---|---|---|
| **National Total** | 140005 | 100.0 |
| Of which: Urban | 84843 | 60.60 |
| Rural | 55162 | 39.40 |
| Of which: Male | 71527 | 51.1 |
| Female | 68478 | 48.9 |
| Of which: Aged 0-15 (under the age of 16) [11] | 24977 | 17.8 |
| Aged 16-59 (under the age of 60) | 89640 | 64.0 |
| Aged 60 and above | 25388 | 18.1 |
| Of which: Aged 65 and above | 17603 | 12.6 |

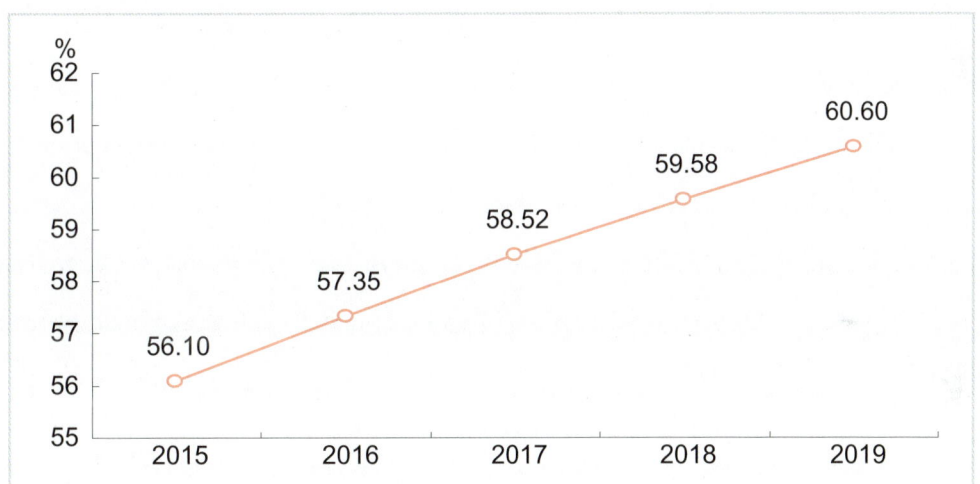

Figure 5: Urbanization Rates of Permanent Residents 2015-2019

At the end of 2019, the number of employed people in China was 774.71 million, and that in urban areas was 442.47 million, accounting for 57.1 percent of the national employed people, 1.1 percentage points higher than the end of 2018. The newly increased employed people in urban areas numbered 13.52 million, 90 thousand less than the previous year. The surveyed urban unemployment rate was 5.2 percent at the year end, and the registered urban unemployment rate was 3.6 percent. The total number of migrant workers[12] in 2019 was 290.77 million, up by 0.8 percent over that of 2018. Specifically, the number of migrant workers who left their hometowns and worked in other places was 174.25 million, up by 0.9 percent, and those who worked in their own localities reached 116.52 million, up by 0.7 percent.

---

11. By the end of 2019, the population aged 0 to 14 (under the age of 15) was 234.92 million and that aged 15 to 59 (under the age of 60) was 911.25 million.

12. The number of migrant workers includes those who are employed outside their villages and towns for more than six months in the year and those who do non-agricultural work in their villages and towns for more than six months in the year.

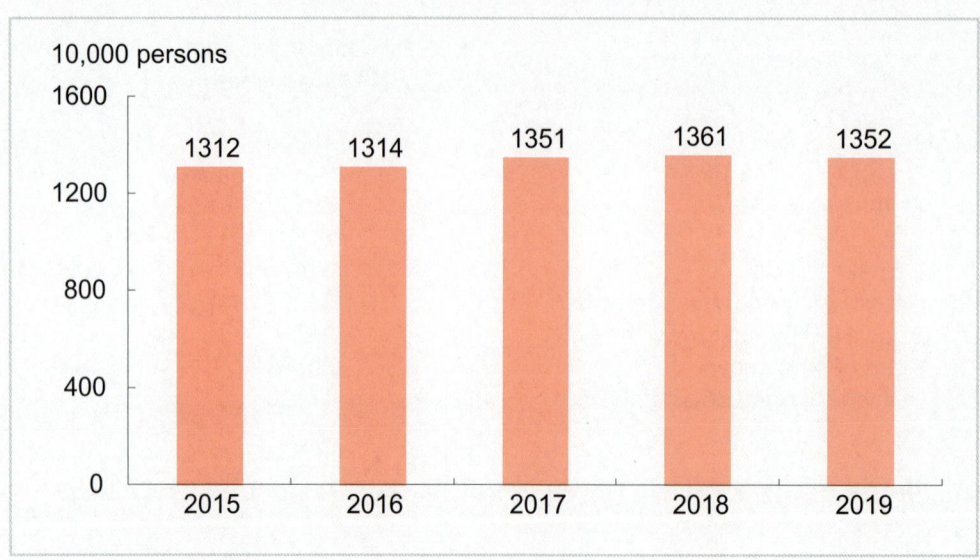

Figure 6: Newly Increased Employed People in Urban Areas 2015-2019

The consumer prices in 2019 went up by 2.9 percent over the previous year. The producer prices for industrial products went down by 0.3 percent and the purchasing prices for industrial producers down by 0.7 percent. The prices for investment in fixed assets increased by 2.6 percent. The producer prices for farm products[13] increased by 14.5 percent. In December, out of the 70 large-and-medium-sized cities, 68 cities experienced a year-on-year rise in sales prices of new commercial residential buildings and two cities experienced a decline.

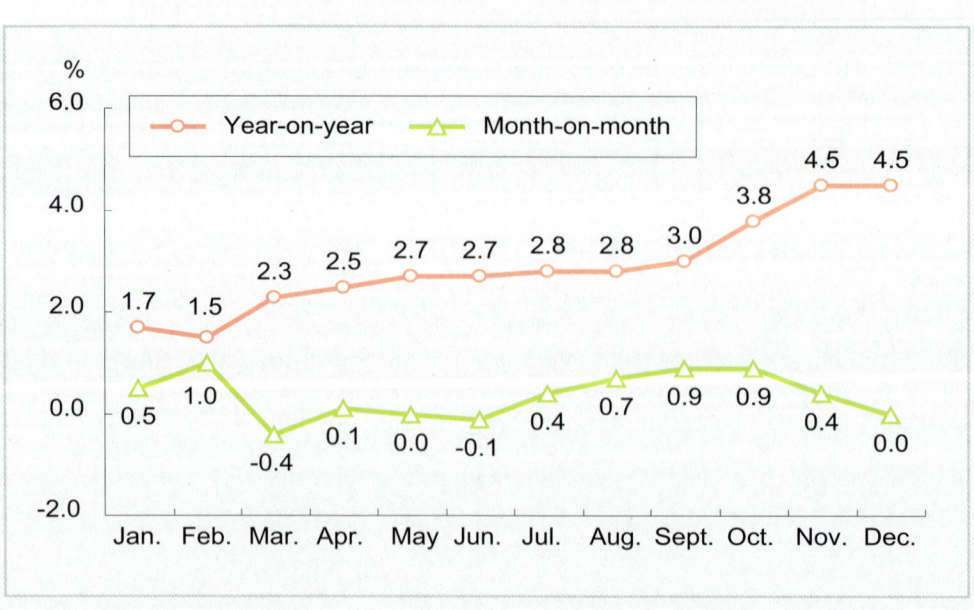

Figure 7: Monthly Changes of Consumer Prices in 2019

---

13. The producer prices for farm products refer to the prices of farm products sold directly by producers.

### Table 2: Changes of Consumer Prices in 2019

Unit: %

| Item | National Average | Urban | Rural |
|---|---|---|---|
| **General level of consumer prices** | **2.9** | **2.8** | **3.2** |
| Of which: Food, tobacco and liquor | 7.0 | 6.7 | 7.9 |
| Clothing | 1.6 | 1.7 | 1.2 |
| Residence[14] | 1.4 | 1.3 | 1.5 |
| Household facilities, articles and services | 0.9 | 0.9 | 0.8 |
| Transportation and telecommunication | -1.7 | -1.8 | -1.4 |
| Education, culture and recreation | 2.2 | 2.3 | 1.9 |
| Health care and medical services | 2.4 | 2.5 | 2.1 |
| Miscellaneous goods and services | 3.4 | 3.5 | 3.1 |

At the end of 2019, China's foreign exchange reserves reached 3,107.9 billion US dollars, an increase of 35.2 billion US dollars compared with that at the end of 2018. The average exchange rate of the year was 6.8985 RMB to 1 USD dollar, depreciated by 4.1 percent over that of 2018.

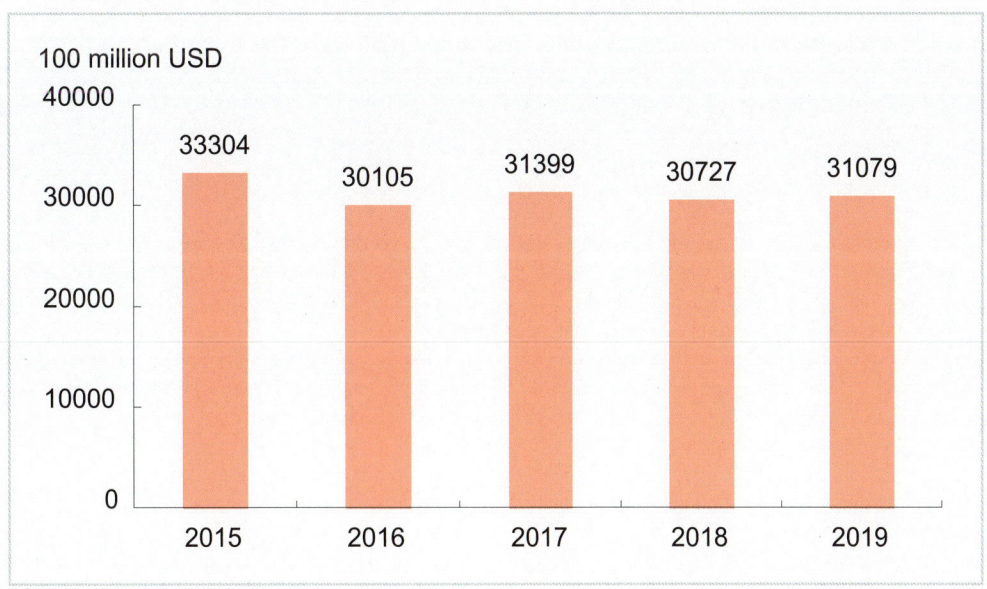

Figure 8: Year-end China's Foreign Exchange Reserves 2015-2019

---

14. The prices for residence include prices for rent, maintenance and management, water, electricity and fuel etc.

The supply-side structural reform was further pushed forward. The national industrial capacity utilization rate[15] in 2019 reached 76.6 percent, 0.1 percentage points higher than the previous year. Specifically, the capacity utilization rate for smelting and pressing of ferrous metals was 80.0 percent, 2.0 percentage points higher than the previous year and that for mining and washing of coal was 70.6 percent, the same as the previous year. The floor space of commercial buildings for sale at the end of 2019 was 498.21 million square meters, 25.93 million square meters less than that at the end of 2018. Of this total, the floor space of the commercial residential buildings for sale was 224.73 million square meters, 26.18 million square meters less. The asset-liability ratio of the industrial enterprises above the designated size at the end of 2019 was 56.6 percent, 0.2 percentage points[16] lower than that at the end of 2018. In 2019, the fixed assets investment (excluding rural households) in education and in ecological protection and treatment of environmental pollution went up by 17.7 percent and 37.2 percent respectively compared with 2018. The reform to streamline administration, delegate powers and improve regulation and services continued to deepen and the vitality of micro entities were enhanced. In 2019, there were 23.77 million market entities newly registered with 20 thousand enterprises newly registered per day on average. At the end of the year, the market entities totaled 120 million. In 2019, the taxes and fees cut reached 2.3 trillion yuan.

The new driving forces continued to grow. Among the industries above the designated size, the value added of the strategic emerging industries[17] grew by 8.4 percent over the previous year and the value added of the high technology manufacturing industry[18] was up by 8.8 percent, accounting for 14.4 percent of that of all industrial enterprises above the designated size. The value added for the manufacture of equipment[19] was up by 6.7 percent, accounting for 32.5 percent of that of all industrial enterprises above the designated size.

---

15. Capacity utilization rate refers to the ratio of the actual production to the production capacity (in terms of value). Actual production refers to the total industrial output value during the enterprise's reporting period. Production capacity refers to the production which can be realized and sustained for a long term under the condition of the supply of labor force, materials, fuel and transportation guaranteed and the production equipment in proper operation.

16. The growth rates and rate changes of financial indicators of industrial enterprises above the designated size in 2019 are calculated on a comparable basis due to adjustments of data coverage in the statistical programmes, statistical law enforcement, removal of duplicated data, corporate reforms and divestiture and the fourth national economic census etc.

17. Industrial strategic emerging industries refer to the related industrial sectors of information technology of new generation, manufacture of high-end equipment, new materials, biotech, new energy vehicles, new energy, energy-saving and environmental protection and digital creative industries. The growth rate of the value-added of the industrial strategic emerging industries in 2019 is calculated on a comparable basis.

18. High technology manufacturing industry includes manufacture of medicine, manufacture of aerospace vehicle and equipment, manufacture of electronic and communication equipment, manufacture of computers and office equipment, manufacture of medical equipment, manufacture of measuring instrument and equipment and manufacture of optical and photographic equipment.

19. Manufacture of equipment includes manufacture of metal products, general purpose equipment, special purpose equipment, automobiles, railway, ship, aerospace and other transport equipment, electrical machinery and apparatus, computers, communication and other electric equipment and measuring instrument and machinery.

Among the service enterprises above the designated size[20], the business revenue of the strategic emerging service industries[21] went up by 12.7 percent compared with the previous year. In 2019, the investment in high technology industries[22] increased by 17.3 percent over the previous year; the investment in industrial technological transformation[23] increased by 9.8 percent. In 2019, the production of service robots reached 3.46 million, up by 38.9 percent compared with the previous year. In 2019, the online retail sales[24] reached 10,632.4 billion yuan, an increase of 16.5 percent over the previous year on a comparable basis.

Regional coordinated development was pushed forward steadily. By regions[25], in 2019, the gross domestic product in the eastern areas was 51,116.1 billion yuan, an increase of 6.2 percent compared with the previous year; the central areas, 21,873.8 billion yuan, up by 7.3 percent; the western areas, 20,518.5 billion yuan, up by 6.7 percent; and the northeastern areas, 5,024.9 billion yuan, up by 4.5 percent. In 2019, the gross domestic product in Beijing-Tianjin-Hebei Region reached 8,458.0 billion yuan, up by 6.1 percent over the previous year; that in the Yangtze River Economic Belt, 45,780.5 billion yuan, up by 6.9 percent; and that in the Yangtze River Delta, 23,725.3 billion yuan, up by 6.4 percent.

Significant achievement has been made in poverty alleviation. By the rural poverty line of annual per capita income of 2,300 yuan (at 2010 constant prices), the number of rural population living in poverty at the end of 2019 was 5.51 million, 11.09 million[26] less compared with that at the end of 2018, and the incidence of

---

20. Service enterprises above the designated size, refer to entities of transport, storage and post, information transmission, software and information technology services, real estate (excluding real estate development and operation), leasing and business services, scientific research and technical services, water conservancy, environment and public facilities management and education, health and social work with annual business revenue of 10 million yuan and above or with 50 employees and above at the end of the year; legal entities of services to households, repair and other services and culture, sports and entertainment with annual business revenue of 5 million and above or with 50 employees and above at the end of the year.

21. Strategic emerging service industries refer to the related service sectors of information technology of new generation, manufacture of high-end equipment, new materials, biotech, new energy vehicles, new energy, energy-saving and environmental protection and digital creative industries, and service industries related to new technology and new entrepreneurship. The growth rate of the business revenue of the strategic emerging service industries in 2019 is calculated on a comparable basis.

22. Investment in high technology industries refers to investment in six high technology manufacturing industries, including the manufacture of medicine and manufacture of aerospace vehicle and equipment, and nine high technology service industries, including information service and e-commerce service.

23. Investment in industrial technological transformation refers to the investment in the improvement of the existing equipment, technologies and production services through new technologies, crafts, equipment and materials so as to achieve intensive development.

24. Online retail sales refer to the retail sales of goods and services realized through internet trading platforms (online platforms mainly in trading physical commodities, including self-built websites and third-party platforms).

25. The eastern areas include 10 provinces and municipalities: Beijing, Tianjin, Hebei, Shanghai, Jiangsu, Zhejiang, Fujian, Shandong, Guangdong and Hainan; the central areas cover 6 provinces: Shanxi, Anhui, Jiangxi, Henan, Hubei and Hunan; the western areas include 12 provinces, autonomous regions and municipalities: Inner Mongolia, Guangxi, Chongqing, Sichuan, Guizhou, Yunnan, Tibet, Shaanxi, Gansu, Qinghai, Ningxia and Xinjiang; the northeastern areas include 3 provinces: Liaoning, Jilin and Heilongjiang.

26. The number of people lifted out of poverty equals the population in poverty in the current year minus that in the previous year. It is also equivalent to the population out of poverty minus the population returning to poverty in the current year.

poverty[27] was 0.6 percent, 1.1 percentage points lower than that of the previous year. In 2019, the per capita disposable income of rural residents in impoverished areas[28] was 11,567 yuan, an increase of 11.5 percent over 2018, or a real increase of 8.0 percent after deducting price factors.

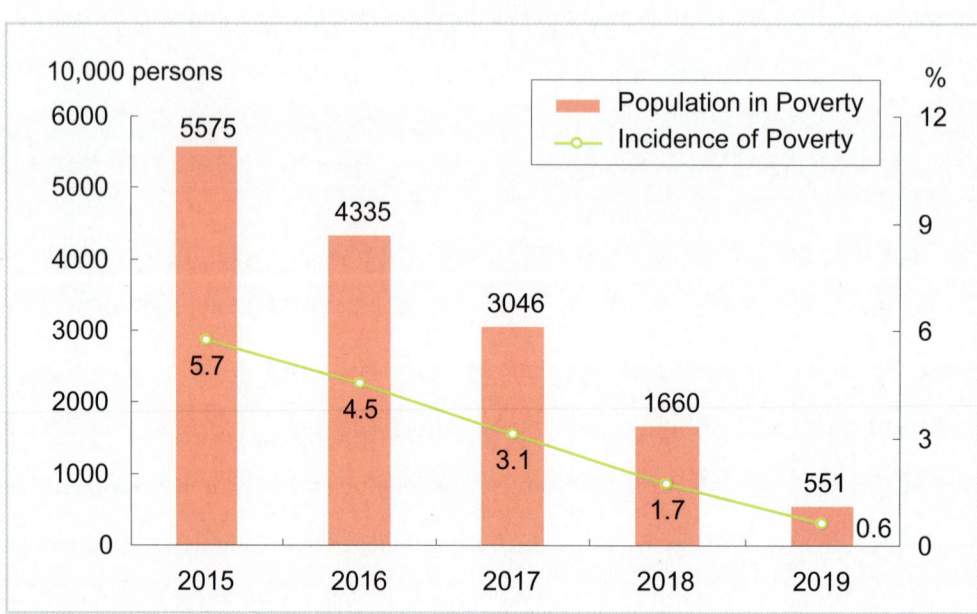

Figure 9: Year-end Rural Population in Poverty and Incidence of Poverty 2015-2019

## II. Agriculture

In 2019, the sown area of grain was 116.06 million hectares, a drop of 0.97 million hectares compared with that in 2018. Of this total, the sown area of wheat was 23.73 million hectares, a decrease of 0.54 million hectares; the sown area of rice was 29.69 million hectares, a decrease of 0.50 million hectares; the sown area of corn was 41.28 million hectares, a decrease of 0.85 million hectares. The sown area of cotton was 3.34 million hectares, a decrease of 20 thousand hectares. The sown area of oil-bearing crops was 12.93 million hectares, up by 60 thousand hectares; the sown area of sugar crops was 1.62 million hectares, down by 10 thousand hectares.

The total output of grain in 2019 was 663.84 million tons, an increase of 5.94 million tons over the

---

27. The incidence of poverty refers to the proportion of population in poverty to targeted population under survey.
28. Impoverished areas cover contiguous poverty-stricken areas and key counties under national poverty alleviation and development program beyond those areas. There were 832 counties altogether. Since 2017, Aksu prefecture in Xinjiang has also been covered in poverty monitoring.

previous year, or up by 0.9 percent. Of this total, the output of summer crops was 141.60 million tons, up by 2.0 percent, and that of the early rice was 26.27 million tons, down by 8.1 percent. The output of autumn grain was 495.97 million tons, up by 1.1 percent. The output of cereal was 613.68 million tons, up by 0.6 percent over 2018, among which the output of rice was 209.61 million tons, down by 1.2 percent; that of wheat was 133.59 million tons, up by 1.6 percent; and that of corn was 260.77 million tons, up by 1.4 percent.

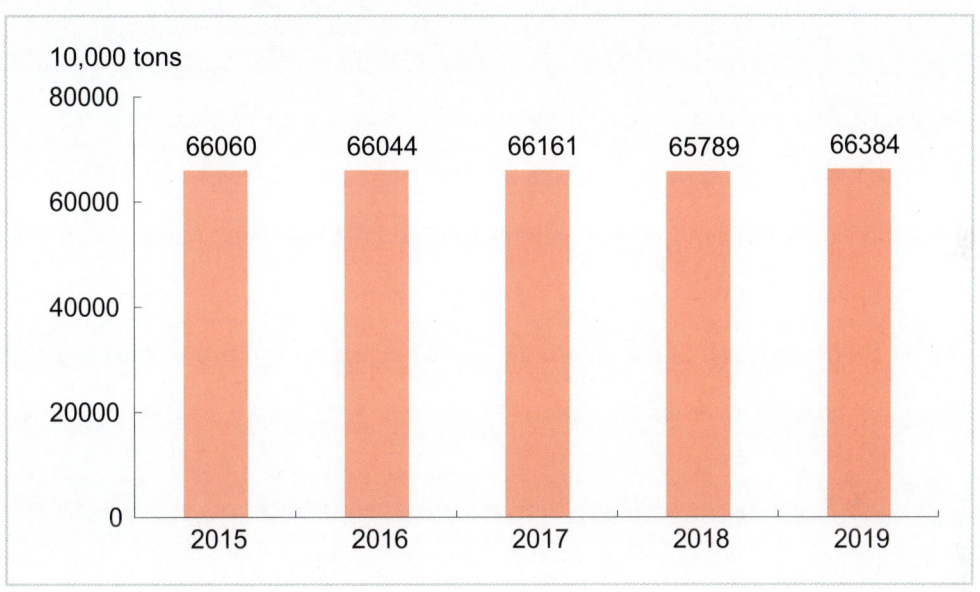

Figure 10: Output of Grain 2015-2019

In 2019, the output of cotton was 5.89 million tons, a decrease of 3.5 percent over the previous year, that of oil-bearing crops was 34.95 million tons, up by 1.8 percent, that of sugar crops was 122.04 million tons, up by 2.2 percent, and that of tea was 2.80 million tons, up by 7.2 percent.

The total output of pork, beef, mutton and poultry in 2019 was 76.49 million tons, down by 10.2 percent over the previous year. Of this total, the output of pork was 42.55 million tons, down by 21.3 percent; that of beef was 6.67 million tons, up by 3.6 percent; that of mutton was 4.88 million tons, up by 2.6 percent; and that of poultry was 22.39 million tons, up by 12.3 percent. The total output of eggs was 33.09 million tons, up by 5.8 percent. The production of milk was 32.01 million tons, up by 4.1 percent. At the end of the year, 310.41 million pigs were registered in the total stocks, down by 27.5 percent, and 544.19 million pigs were slaughtered, down by 21.6 percent.

The total output of aquatic products in 2019 was 64.50 million tons, down by 0.1 percent over the previous year. Of this total, the output of cultured aquatic products was 50.50 million tons, up by 1.0 percent;

and that of fished aquatic products was 14.00 million tons, down by 5.0 percent.

The total production of timber for 2019 reached 90.28 million cubic meters, up by 2.5 percent over the previous year.

In 2019, over 0.27 million hectares of farmland were newly equipped with irrigation systems and another 1.46 million hectares of farmland was newly equipped with water-saving irrigation systems.

### III. Industry and Construction

In 2019, the total value added of the industrial sector was 31,710.9 billion yuan, up by 5.7 percent over the previous year. The value added of industrial enterprises above the designated size increased by 5.7 percent. Of the industrial enterprises above the designated size, in terms of ownership, the value added of the state-holding enterprises grew by 4.8 percent, that of the share-holding enterprises up by 6.8 percent, that of the enterprises funded by foreign investors and investors from Hong Kong, Macao and Taiwan up by 2.0 percent and that of private enterprises up by 7.7 percent. In terms of sectors, the value added of the mining industry was up by 5.0 percent, that of manufacturing up by 6.0 percent and that of production and supply of electricity, heat power, gas and water up by 7.0 percent.

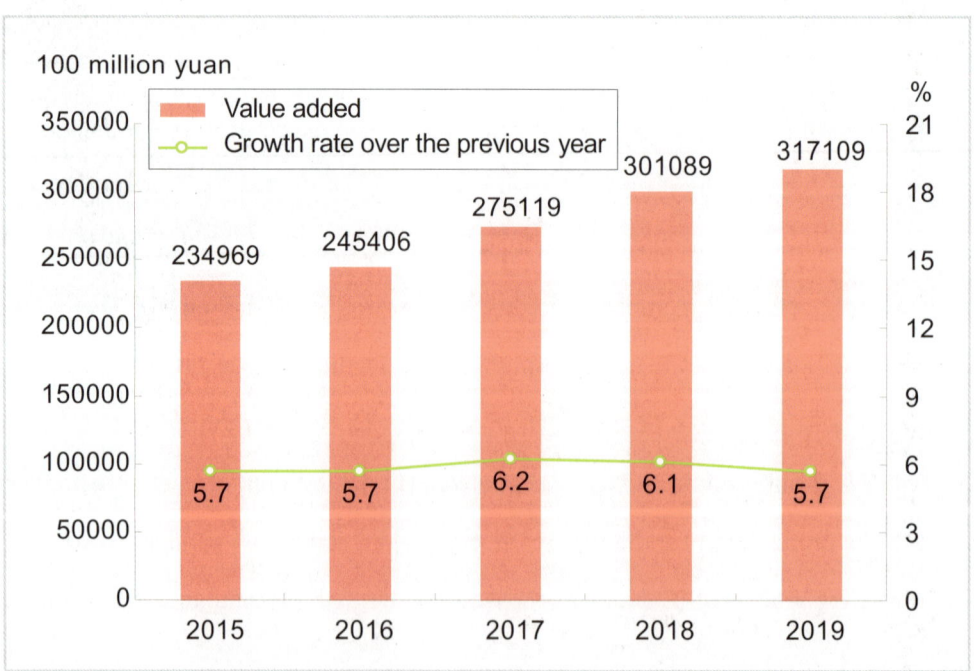

Figure 11: Value Added and Growth Rates of Industrial Enterprises 2015-2019[29]

---

29. See Note 2.

## Table 3: Output of Major Industrial Products and Growth Rates in 2019[30]

| Product | Unit | Output | Increase over 2018 (%) |
|---|---|---|---|
| Yarn | 10000 tons | 2892.1 | -6.1 |
| Cloth | 100 million meters | 575.6 | -17.6 |
| Chemical fiber | 10000 tons | 5952.8 | 9.9 |
| Refined sugar (final product) | 10000 tons | 1389.4 | 15.9 |
| Cigarettes | 100 million | 23642.5 | 1.1 |
| Color TV sets | 10000 | 18999.1 | -3.5 |
| Of which: LCD TV sets | 10000 | 18689.7 | -1.5 |
| Household refrigerators | 10000 | 7904.3 | 6.3 |
| Air conditioners | 10000 | 21866.2 | 4.3 |
| Primary energy output | 100 million tons of standard coal equivalent | 39.7 | 5.1 |
| Coal | 100 million tons | 38.5 | 4.0 |
| Crude petroleum oil | 10000 tons | 19101.4 | 0.9 |
| Natural gas | 100 million cubic meters | 1761.7 | 10.0 |
| Electricity | 100 million kilowatt-hours | 75034.3 | 4.7 |
| Of which: Thermal power[31] | 100 million kilowatt-hours | 52201.5 | 2.4 |
| Hydropower | 100 million kilowatt-hours | 13044.4 | 5.9 |
| Nuclear-power | 100 million kilowatt-hours | 3483.5 | 18.3 |
| Crude steel | 10000 tons | 99634.2 | 7.2 |
| Rolled steel[32] | 10000 tons | 120477.4 | 6.3 |
| Ten kinds of nonferrous metals | 10000 tons | 5866.0 | 2.2 |
| Of which: Refined copper (copper) | 10000 tons | 978.4 | 5.5 |
| Aluminum electrolyze | 10000 tons | 3504.4 | -2.2 |
| Cement | 100 million tons | 23.5 | 4.9 |
| Sulfuric acid (100%) | 10000 tons | 8935.7 | -1.3 |
| Caustic soda (100%) | 10000 tons | 3464.4 | -0.3 |
| Ethylene | 10000 tons | 2052.3 | 10.2 |
| Chemical fertilizers (100 percent equivalent) | 10000 tons | 5731.2 | 6.1 |
| Power generation equipment | 10000 kilowatts | 9274.1 | -14.9 |
| Motor vehicles | 10000 | 2552.8 | -8.3 |
| Of which: Basic passenger cars (cars) | 10000 | 1018.2 | -16.4 |
| Sport utility vehicles (SUVs) | 10000 | 876.0 | -3.6 |
| Large and medium tractors | 10000 | 27.8 | 5.9 |
| Integrated circuits | 100 million pieces | 2018.2 | 8.9 |
| Program-controlled switchboards | 10000 lines | 790.5 | -23.7 |
| Mobile telephones | 10000 | 170100.6 | -5.5 |
| Micro computer equipment | 10000 | 34163.2 | 8.2 |
| Industrial robots | 10000 sets | 17.7 | -3.1 |

30. Output data of some products were revised in 2018 based on the results of the fourth national economic census; the growth rates of output in 2019 are calculated on a comparable basis.
31. Thermal power refers to electricity generated by coal, oil, gas, residual heat, pressure and gas, waste incineration and biomass.
32. The data include 252.00 million tons of steel which has been reprocessed among enterprises.

In 2019, of the industrial enterprises above the designated size, the value added for processing of food from agricultural and sideline products was up by 1.9 percent over the previous year; for textile industry up by 1.3 percent; for manufacture of raw chemical materials and chemical products up by 4.7 percent; for manufacture of non-metallic mineral products up by 8.9 percent; for smelting and pressing of ferrous metals up by 9.9 percent; for manufacture of general purpose machinery up by 4.3 percent; for manufacture of special purpose machinery up by 6.9 percent; for manufacture of automobiles up by 1.8 percent; for manufacture of electrical machinery and apparatus up by 10.7 percent; for manufacture of computers, communication equipment and other electronic equipment up by 9.3 percent; for production and supply of electricity and heat power up by 6.5 percent.

By the end of 2019, the installed power generation capacity was 2,010.66 million kilowatts, up by 5.8 percent over that at the end of 2018, among which[33] the installed thermal power generation capacity was 1,190.55 million kilowatts, up by 4.1 percent; the installed hydropower generation capacity was 356.40 million kilowatts, up by 1.1 percent; the installed nuclear power generation capacity was 48.74 million kilowatts, up by 9.1 percent. The installed grid-connected wind power generation capacity was 210.05 million kilowatts, up by 14.0 percent and the installed grid-connected solar power generation capacity was 204.68 million kilowatts, up by 17.4 percent.

In 2019, the profits made by industrial enterprises above the designated size were 6,199.6 billion yuan, down by 3.3 percent[34] over the previous year. By ownership, the profits of state-holding enterprises were 1,635.6 billion yuan, down by 12.0 percent over the previous year; those of share-holding enterprises were 4,528.4 billion yuan, down by 2.9 percent; those of enterprises funded by foreign investors or investors from Hong Kong, Macao and Taiwan were 1,558.0 billion yuan, down by 3.6 percent; and those of private enterprises were 1,818.2 billion yuan, up by 2.2 percent. In terms of different sectors, the profits of mining were 527.5 billion yuan, up by 1.7 percent over the previous year; those of manufacturing were 5,190.4 billion yuan, down by 5.2 percent; and those of the production and supply of electricity, heat power, gas and water were 481.6 billion yuan, up by 15.4 percent. In 2019, the cost for per-hundred-yuan business revenue of the industrial enterprises above the designated size was 84.08 yuan, or 0.18 yuan more than that of 2018; the profit rate of the business revenue was 5.86 percent, down by 0.43 percentage points.

---

33. Some installed power generation capacity was not listed (e.g. geothermal).
34. See note 16.

In 2019, the value added of construction enterprises in China was 7,090.4 billion yuan, up by 5.6 percent over the previous year. The profits made by construction enterprises qualified for general contracts and specialized contracts reached 838.1 billion yuan, up by 5.1 percent over the previous year, of which the profits made by state-holding enterprises were 258.5 billion yuan, up by 14.5 percent.

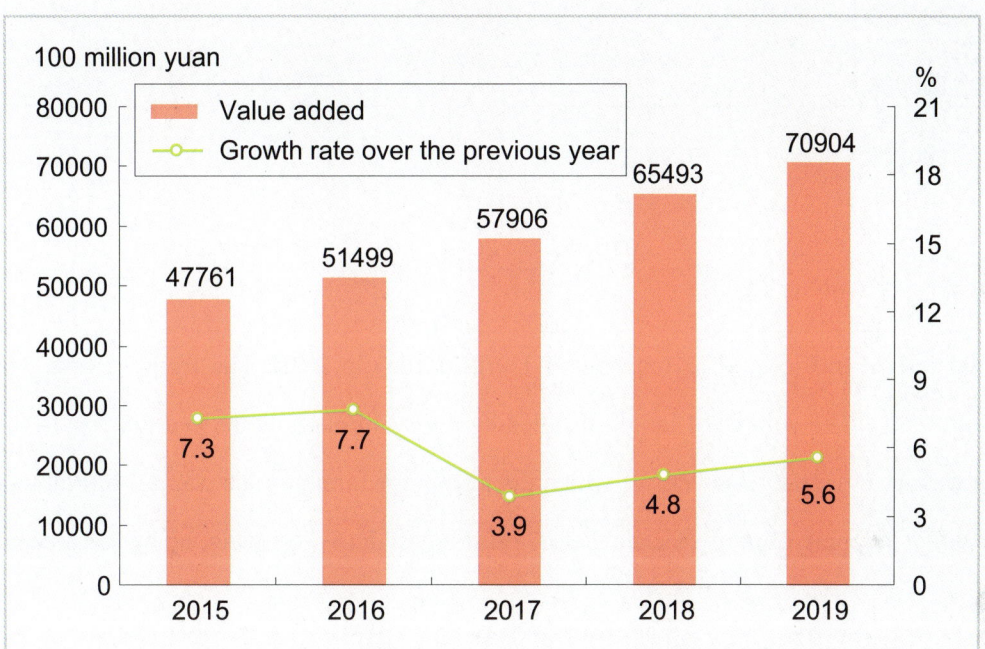

Figure 12: Value Added and Growth Rates of Construction Industry 2015-2019[35]

## IV. Service Sector

In 2019, the value added of the wholesale and retail trades was 9,584.6 billion yuan, up by 5.7 percent over the previous year; that of transport, storage and post was 4,280.2 billion yuan, up by 7.1 percent; that of hotels and catering services was 1,804.0 billion yuan, up by 6.3 percent; that of financial intermediation was 7,707.7 billion yuan, up by 7.2 percent; that of real estate was 6,963.1 billion yuan, up by 3.0 percent; that of information transmission, software and information technology services was 3,269.0 billion yuan, up by 18.7 percent; and that of leasing and business services was 3,293.3 billion yuan, up by 8.7 percent. In 2019, the business revenue of service enterprises above the designated size grew by 9.4 percent over the previous year, and the operating profits grew by 5.4 percent.

---

35. See Note 2.

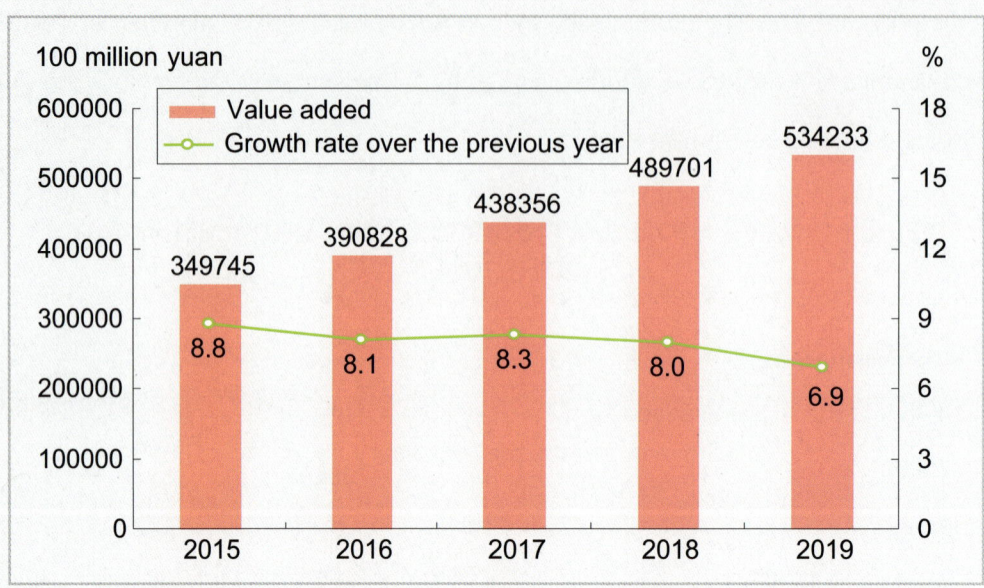

Figure 13: Value Added and Growth Rates of Service Sector 2015-2019[36]

The total freight traffic in 2019 reached 47.1 billion tons in 2019. The freight flows were 19,929.0 billion ton-kilometers. The volume of freight handled by ports[37] throughout the year totaled 14.0 billion tons, up by 5.7 percent over the previous year, of which the freight for foreign trade was 4.3 billion tons, up by 4.7 percent. Container shipping of ports reached 261.07 million standard containers, up by 4.4 percent.

Table 4: Freight Traffic by All Means of Transportation and Growth Rates in 2019[38]

| Item | Unit | Volume | Increase over 2018(%) |
|---|---|---|---|
| **Total freight traffic** | 100 million tons | 470.6 | — |
| Railways | 100 million tons | 43.2 | 7.2 |
| Highways | 100 million tons | 343.5 | — |
| Waterways | 100 million tons | 74.7 | 6.3 |
| Civil aviation | 10 000 tons | 753.2 | 2.0 |
| Pipelines | 100 million tons | 9.1 | 1.8 |
| **Freight flows** | 100 million ton-kilometers | 199289.5 | — |
| Railways | 100 million ton-kilometers | 30074.7 | 4.4 |
| Highways | 100 million ton-kilometers | 59636.4 | — |
| Waterways | 100 million ton-kilometers | 103963.0 | 5.0 |
| Civil aviation | 100 million ton-kilometers | 263.2 | 0.3 |
| Pipelines | 100 million ton-kilometers | 5352.2 | 1.0 |

36. See Note 2.
37. In 2019, the statistical coverage of ports expanded from ports above the designated size to all ports; the growth rates of relevant indicators are calculated on a comparable basis.
38. The Ministry of Transport adjusted the coverage of the freight traffic and freight flow of the highways in 2019 based on the ad hoc survey so the data are incomparable with the previous year.

In 2019, the total passenger traffic[39] reached 17.6 billion person-times, down by 1.9 percent over 2018, and the passenger flows were 3,534.9 billion person-kilometers, up by 3.3 percent.

**Table 5: Passenger Traffic by All Means of Transportation and Growth Rates in 2019**

| Item | Unit | Volume | Increase over 2018(%) |
|---|---|---|---|
| **Total passenger traffic** | 100 million person-times | 176.0 | -1.9 |
| Railways | 100 million person-times | 36.6 | 8.4 |
| Highways | 100 million person-times | 130.1 | -4.8 |
| Waterways | 100 million person-times | 2.7 | -2.6 |
| Civil aviation | 100 million person-times | 6.6 | 7.9 |
| **Passenger flows** | 100 million person-kilometers | 35349.1 | 3.3 |
| Railways | 100 million person-kilometers | 14706.6 | 4.0 |
| Highways | 100 million person-kilometers | 8857.1 | -4.6 |
| Waterways | 100 million person-kilometers | 80.2 | 0.8 |
| Civil aviation | 100 million person-kilometers | 11705.1 | 9.3 |

The total number of motor vehicles for civilian use reached 261.50 million (including 7.62 million tri-wheel motor vehicles and low-speed trucks) by the end of 2019, up by 21.22 million over that at the end of 2018, of which the privately-owned vehicles numbered 226.35 million, an increase of 19.05 million. The total number of cars for civilian use was 146.44 million, an increase of 11.93 million, of which the privately-owned cars numbered 137.01 million, an increase of 11.12 million.

The turnover of post services[40] totaled 1,623.0 billion yuan, up by 31.5 percent over the previous year. In 2019, the number of mail delivery was 2.17 billion; that of parcel delivery was 20 million; and that of express delivery was 63.52 billion with a revenue reaching 749.8 billion yuan. The turnover of telecommunication services[41] totaled 10,678.9 billion yuan, up by 62.9 percent over the previous year. By the end of 2019, there were 1,792.38 million phone subscribers in China, 1,601.34 million of which were mobile phone subscribers. Mobile phone coverage rose to 114.4 sets per 100 persons. The number of fixed broadband internet users[42] reached 449.28 million, an increase of 41.90 million over the end of the previous year. Of this total, fixed

---

39. The total passenger traffic includes passenger traffic by railways, highways, waterways and civil aviation for commercial purpose, of which traffic by highways accounted for more than 70 percent. Over recent years, the revolution of people's travel methods has brought about the fast growth of road trips, online car hailing and carpooling, which has caused a decline of the passenger traffic by highways, as well as the total passenger traffic.
40. The turnover of post services is calculated at constant prices of 2010.
41. The turnover of telecommunication services is calculated at constant prices of 2015.
42. Fixed broadband internet users refer to those who subscribed to the telecommunication enterprises and access the Internet through xDSL, FTTx+LAN, FTTH/0 and other broadband access ways as well as general dedicated lines at the end of the reporting period.

fiber-optic broadband internet users[43] amounted to 417.40 million, an increase of 49.07 million. The mobile internet traffic in 2019 was 122.0 billion gigabytes, up by 71.6 percent over the previous year. Software revenue from software and information technology services industry[44] in 2019 was 7,176.8 billion yuan, up by 15.4 percent over 2018 on a comparable basis.

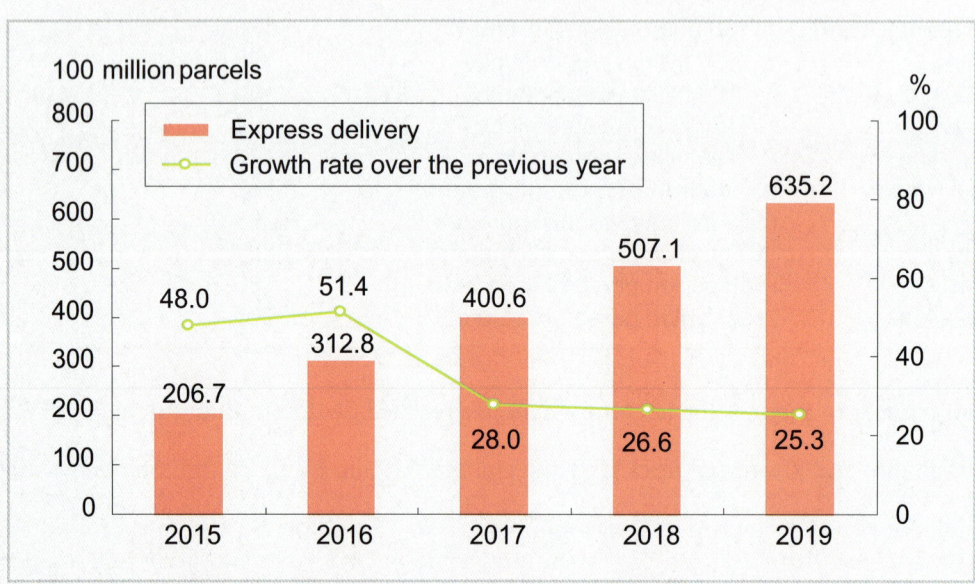

Figure 14: Express Delivery and Growth Rates 2015-2019

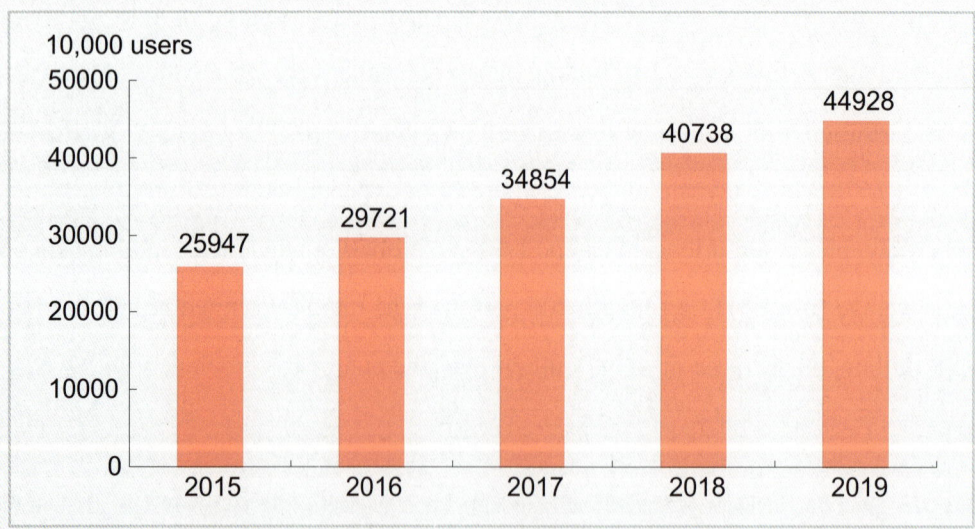

Figure 15: Year-end Number of Fixed Broadband Internet Users 2015-2019

---

43. Fixed fiber-optic broadband internet users refer to those who subscribed to the telecommunication enterprises and access the Internet through FTTH or FTT0 at the end of the reporting period.

44. Software and information technology services industry includes software development, integrated circuit design, information system integration and internet of things technology services, operation maintenance services, information processing and storage support services, IT consulting services, digital content services and other IT services industry.

## V. Domestic Trade

In 2019, the total retail sales of consumer goods reached 41,164.9 billion yuan, a growth of 8.0 percent over the previous year. An analysis on different areas showed that the retail sales of consumer goods in urban areas stood at 35,131.7 billion yuan, up by 7.9 percent, and that in rural areas reached 6,033.2 billion yuan, up by 9.0 percent. Grouped by consumption patterns, the retail sales of commodities was 36,492.8 billion yuan, up by 7.9 percent, and that of catering industry was 4,672.1 billion yuan, up by 9.4 percent.

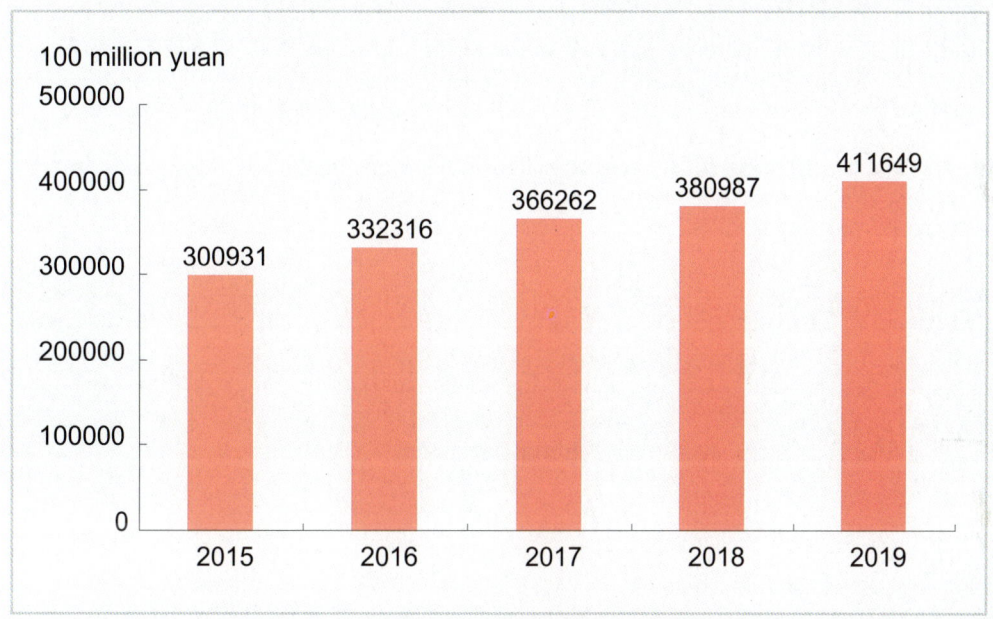

Figure 16: Total Retail Sales of Consumer Goods 2015-2019

Of the total retail sales of commodities by enterprises above the designated size, the year-on-year growth of retail sales for grain, oil and food went up by 10.2 percent; beverage up by 10.4 percent; tobacco and liquor up by 7.4 percent; clothes, shoes, hats and textiles up by 2.9 percent; cosmetics up by 12.6 percent; gold, silver and jewelry up by 0.4 percent; daily necessities up by 13.9 percent; household appliances and audio-video equipment up by 5.6 percent; traditional Chinese and western medicines up by 9.0 percent; cultural and office appliances up by 3.3 percent; furniture up by 5.1 percent; telecommunication equipment up by 8.5 percent; building and decoration materials up by 2.8 percent; petroleum and petroleum products up by 1.2 percent; and motor vehicles down by 0.8 percent.

In 2019, the online retail sales of physical goods were 8,523.9 billion yuan, up by 19.5 percent over the previous year on a comparable basis, accounting for 20.7 percent of the total retail sales of consumer goods, or 2.3 percentage points higher than that of 2018.

## VI. Investment in Fixed Assets

The total investment in fixed assets[45] of the country in 2019 was 56,087.4 billion yuan, up by 5.1 percent over the previous year. Of the total, the investment in fixed assets (excluding rural households) was 55,147.8 billion yuan, up by 5.4 percent. By regions[46], the investment in eastern areas was up by 4.1 percent over the previous year, central areas up by 9.5 percent, western areas up by 5.6 percent, and northeastern areas down by 3.0 percent.

In the investment in fixed assets (excluding rural households), the investment in the primary industry was 1,263.3 billion yuan, up by 0.6 percent over the previous year; that in the secondary industry was 16,307.0 billion yuan, up by 3.2 percent; and that in the tertiary industry was 37,577.5 billion yuan, up by 6.5 percent. The private investment in fixed assets[47] was 31,115.9 billion yuan, up by 4.7 percent. The investment in infrastructure[48] saw an increase of 3.8 percent. The investment in the six major high energy consuming industries grew by 4.7 percent.

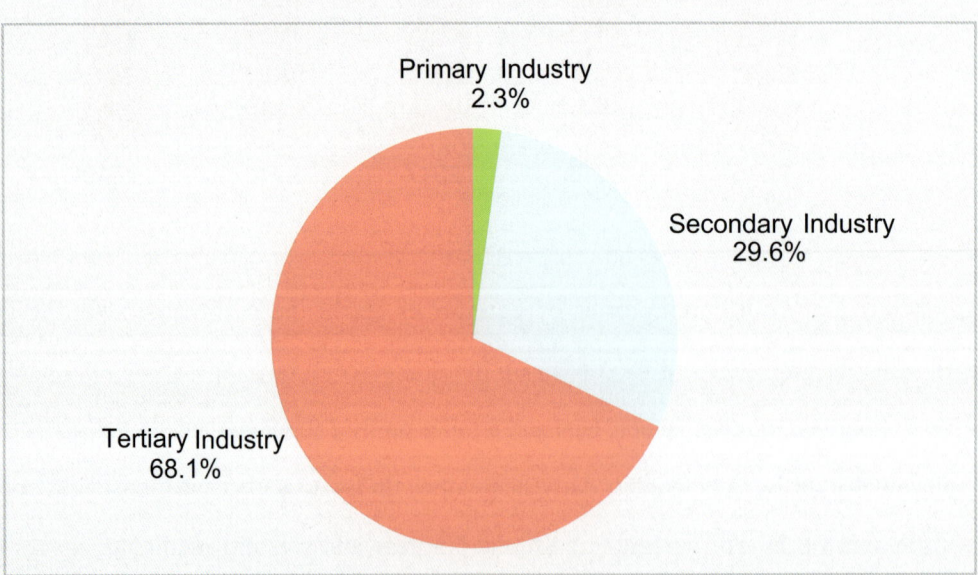

Figure 17: Shares of Investment in Fixed Assets of the Three Industries (Excluding Rural Households) in 2019

---

45. The figure of the investment in fixed assets in 2018 was revised according to the results of the fourth national economic census, statistical law enforcement and the statistical survey programmes. The growth rates in 2019 are calculated on a comparable basis.
46. See Note 25.
47. Private investment in fixed assets refers to investment in the construction or purchase of fixed assets by domestic collective, private and individual-owned enterprises or organizations or their holding enterprises (with absolute holding and relative holding enterprises).
48. Investment in infrastructure includes transportation, postal service, telecommunication, radio, TV and satellite transmission, internet and related services, water conservancy, environment and public facilities management.

### Table 6: Growth Rates of Investment in Fixed Assets (Excluding Rural Households) by Sectors in 2019

| Sector | Increase over 2018 (%) | Sector | Increase over 2018 (%) |
|---|---|---|---|
| Total | 5.4 | Financial Intermediation | 10.4 |
| Agriculture, Forestry, Animal Husbandry and Fishery | 0.7 | Real Estate[49] | 9.1 |
|  |  | Leasing and Business Services | 15.8 |
| Mining | 24.1 | Scientific Research and Technical Services | 17.9 |
| Manufacturing | 3.1 | Water Conservancy, Environment and Public Facilities Management | 2.9 |
| Production and Supply of Electricity, Heat Power, Gas and Water | 4.5 |  |  |
| Construction | -19.8 | Services to Households, Repair and Other Services | -9.1 |
| Wholesale and Retail Trades | -15.9 | Education | 17.7 |
| Transport, Storage and Post | 3.4 | Health and Social Service | 5.3 |
| Hotels and Catering Services | -1.2 | Culture, Sports and Entertainment | 13.9 |
| Information Transmission, Software and Information Technology Services | 8.6 | Public Management, Social Security and Social Organizations | -15.6 |

### Table 7: Newly Increased Production and Operation Capacity through Fixed Assets Investment in 2019

| Item | Unit | Volume |
|---|---|---|
| Newly increased power transformer equipment with a capacity of over 220 kilovolts | 10000 kilovolt-amperes | 23042 |
| New railways put into operation | kilometer | 8489 |
| Of which: high-speed railways[50] | kilometer | 5474 |
| Extended or new double-track railways put into operation | kilometer | 6448 |
| Electrified railways put into operation | kilometer | 7919 |
| Length of New and rebuilt highways | kilometer | 327626 |
| Of which: Expressways | kilometer | 8313 |
| New throughput capacity of berths for over 10,000-tonnage ships | 10000 tons/year | 12022 |
| New civil transportation airports | - | 3 |
| New lines of optical-fiber cables | 10000 km | 434 |

49. The investment in real estate includes the investment in real estate development, construction of buildings for own use, property management, intermediary services and other real estate investment.

50. High-speed railways refer to railways with a maximum operating speed of 200 km/h and above and railways with a maximum operating speed less than 200 km/h but only for high speed trains.

In 2019, the investment in real estate development was 13,219.4 billion yuan, up by 9.9 percent over the previous year. Of this total, the investment in residential buildings reached 9,707.1 billion yuan, an increase of 13.9 percent, that in office buildings was 616.3 billion yuan, up by 2.8 percent, and that in buildings for commercial business was 1,322.6 billion yuan, down by 6.7 percent.

In 2019, 3.16 million housing units were started to be rebuilt in rundown urban areas nationwide. The number of housing units rebuilt in rundown areas was 2.54 million. In rural areas of China, among the poverty-stricken households that had their economic status registered at the local governments, 638 thousand[51] of them witnessed their dilapidated houses rebuilt or renovated in 2019.

**Table 8: Main Indicators for Real Estate Development and Sales and Their Growth Rates in 2019**

| Item | Unit | Volume | Increase over 2018 (%) |
| --- | --- | --- | --- |
| Value of Investment | 100 million RMB | 132194 | 9.9 |
| Of which: residential buildings | 100 million RMB | 97071 | 13.9 |
| Floor space of buildings under construction | 10,000 square meters | 893821 | 8.7 |
| Of which: residential buildings | 10,000 square meters | 627673 | 10.1 |
| Floor space of buildings newly started | 10,000 square meters | 227154 | 8.5 |
| Of which: residential buildings | 10,000 square meters | 167463 | 9.2 |
| Floor space of buildings completed | 10,000 square meters | 95942 | 2.6 |
| Of which: residential buildings | 10,000 square meters | 68011 | 3.0 |
| Floor space of commercial buildings sold | 10,000 square meters | 171558 | -0.1 |
| Of which: residential buildings | 10,000 square meters | 150144 | 1.5 |
| Funds for investment this year | 100 million RMB | 178609 | 7.6 |
| Of which: domestic loans | 100 million RMB | 25229 | 5.1 |
| individual mortgage | 100 million RMB | 27281 | 15.1 |

### VII. Foreign Economic Relations

The total value of imports and exports of goods in 2019 reached 31,550.5 billion yuan, up by 3.4 percent over that of the previous year. Of this total, the value of goods exported was 17,234.2 billion yuan, up by 5.0 percent; the value of goods imported was 14,316.2 billion yuan, up by 1.6 percent. The surplus of trade in goods reached 2,918.0 billion yuan, up by 593.2 billion yuan over that of the previous year. The total value

---

51. The figure is the number of housing units of the poverty-stricken rural households with their economic status registered at the local governments that were started to be rebuilt or renovated by the end of 2019, financed by the central government budget.

of imports and exports between China and countries along the Belt and Road[52] was 9,269.0 billion yuan, an increase of 10.8 percent over that of the previous year. Of the total, the value of goods exported was 5,258.5 billion yuan, an increase of 13.2 percent; that of goods imported was 4,010.5 billion yuan, an increase of 7.9 percent.

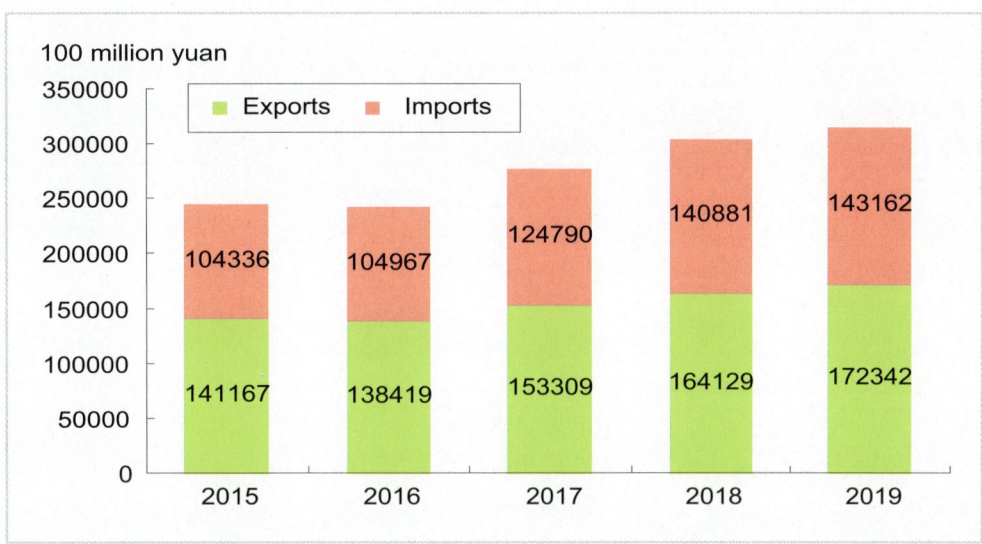

Figure 18: Imports and Exports of Goods 2015-2019

Table 9: Total Value of Import and Export of Goods and the Growth Rates in 2019

| Item | Value (100 million yuan) | Increase over 2018 (%) |
|---|---|---|
| **Total value of import and export of goods** | 315505 | 3.4 |
| Exports | 172342 | 5.0 |
| Of which: General trade | 99546 | 7.8 |
| Processing trade | 50729 | -3.7 |
| Of which: Mechanical and electronic products | 100631 | 4.4 |
| High & new technology products | 50427 | 2.1 |
| Imports | 143162 | 1.6 |
| Of which: General trade | 86599 | 3.1 |
| Processing trade | 28778 | -7.4 |
| Of which: Mechanical and electronic products | 62596 | -1.8 |
| High & new technology products | 43978 | -0.8 |
| **Trade surplus** | 29180 | — |

---

52. The Belt and Road refers to the Silk Road Economic Belt and the 21st Century Maritime Silk Road.

### Table 10: Main Export Commodities in Volume and Value and the Growth Rates in 2019

| Item | Unit | Volume | Increase over 2018 (%) | Value (100 million yuan) | Increase over 2018(%) |
|---|---|---|---|---|---|
| Rolled steel | 10000 tons | 6429 | -7.3 | 3699 | -7.1 |
| Textile yarns and textile articles | — | — | — | 8283 | 5.5 |
| Clothes and clothing accessories | — | — | — | 10447 | 0.3 |
| Footwear | 10000 tons | 451 | 0.6 | 3290 | 6.3 |
| Furniture and parts | — | — | — | 3730 | 5.3 |
| Luggage and similar containers | 10000 tons | 307 | -2.9 | 1878 | 5.1 |
| Toys | — | — | — | 2152 | 29.6 |
| Plastic articles | 10000 tons | 1424 | 8.5 | 3333 | 16.2 |
| Integrated circuits | 100 million pieces | 2187 | 0.7 | 7008 | 25.3 |
| Automatic data processing machines and components | 10000 sets | 148430 | 0.8 | 11415 | 0.5 |
| Handheld mobiles and car telephones | 10000 sets | 99433 | -11.1 | 8611 | -7.8 |
| Containers | 10000 units | 242 | -29.0 | 459 | -33.0 |
| Liquid crystal display panels | 10000 units | 150780 | -14.2 | 1475 | -3.4 |
| Motor vehicles | 10000 sets | 122 | 6.1 | 1049 | 8.0 |

### Table 11: Main Import Commodities in Volume and Value and the Growth Rates in 2019

| Item | Unit | Volume | Increase over 2018 (%) | Value (100 million yuan) | Increase over 2018 (%) |
|---|---|---|---|---|---|
| Cereals and cereals flour | 10000 tons | 1785 | -12.8 | 358 | -7.0 |
| Soybean | 10000 tons | 8851 | 0.5 | 2437 | -2.6 |
| Edible vegetable oil | 10000 tons | 953 | 51.5 | 438 | 39.9 |
| Iron ore and concentrate | 10000 tons | 106895 | 0.5 | 6995 | 39.6 |
| Coal and lignite | 10000 tons | 29967 | 6.3 | 1605 | -1.1 |
| Crude oil | 10000 tons | 50572 | 9.5 | 16627 | 4.6 |
| Petroleum products refined | 10000 tons | 3056 | -8.7 | 1175 | -11.7 |
| Natural gas | 10000 tons | 9656 | 6.9 | 2875 | 12.8 |
| Plastics in primary forms | 10000 tons | 3691 | 12.4 | 3670 | -1.3 |
| Paper pulp | 10000 tons | 2720 | 9.7 | 1178 | -9.3 |
| Rolled steel | 10000 tons | 1230 | -6.5 | 973 | -10.2 |
| Unwrought copper and its alloys | 10000 tons | 498 | -6.0 | 2240 | -9.2 |
| Integrated circuits | 100 million pieces | 4451 | 6.6 | 21079 | 2.4 |
| Motor vehicles | 10000 sets | 105 | -7.6 | 3332 | 0.0 |

### Table 12: Imports and Exports of Goods by Major Countries and Regions, the Growth Rates and Proportions in 2019

| Country or region | Exports (100 million yuan) | Increase over 2018 (%) | Proportion of the total (%) | Imports (100 million yuan) | Increase over 2018 (%) | Proportion of the total (%) |
|---|---|---|---|---|---|---|
| European Union | 29564 | 9.6 | 17.2 | 19063 | 5.5 | 13.3 |
| ASEAN | 24797 | 17.8 | 14.4 | 19456 | 9.8 | 13.6 |
| United States | 28865 | -8.7 | 16.7 | 8454 | -17.1 | 5.9 |
| Japan | 9875 | 1.7 | 5.7 | 11837 | -0.6 | 8.3 |
| Hong Kong, China | 19243 | -3.6 | 11.2 | 626 | 10.9 | 0.4 |
| Republic of Korea | 7648 | 6.6 | 4.4 | 11960 | -11.4 | 8.4 |
| Taiwan, China | 3799 | 18.3 | 2.2 | 11934 | 1.9 | 8.3 |
| Brazil | 2453 | 10.8 | 1.4 | 5501 | 7.4 | 3.8 |
| Russia | 3434 | 8.5 | 2.0 | 4208 | 7.5 | 2.9 |
| India | 5156 | 2.1 | 3.0 | 1239 | -0.2 | 0.9 |
| South Africa | 1141 | 6.4 | 0.7 | 1784 | -0.8 | 1.2 |

The total value of imports and exports of services[53] in 2019 was 5,415.3 billion yuan, up by 2.8 percent over that of the previous year. The export value of services was 1,956.4 billion yuan, up by 8.9 percent. The import value of services was 3,458.9 billion yuan, down by 0.4 percent. The trade deficit in imports and exports of services was 1,502.5 billion yuan.

The year 2019 witnessed the establishment of 40,888 enterprises (excluding banking, securities and insurance) with foreign direct investment, down by 32.5 percent over that of the previous year, and the foreign direct investment actually utilized totaled 941.5 billion yuan, up by 5.8 percent, or 138.1 billion US dollars, up by 2.4 percent. Specifically, there were 5,591 newly established enterprises receiving direct investment from countries along the Belt and Road, up by 24.8 percent; and foreign capital directly invested in China (including the investment in China via some free ports) reached 57.6 billion yuan, up by 36.0 percent, or 8.4 billion US dollars, up by 30.6 percent. In 2019, the foreign investment actually utilized by high technology industry reached 266.0 billion yuan, up by 25.6 percent, or 39.1 billion US dollars, up by 21.7 percent.

---

53. The imports and exports of services are calculated according to the sixth edition of *Balance of Payments and International Investment Position Manual* (BPM6), and the growth rate is calculated on a comparable basis.

### Table 13: Total Value of Foreign Direct Investment (Excluding Banking, Securities and Insurance) and the Growth Rates in 2019

| Sector | Enterprises | Increase over 2018 (%) | Actually Utilized Value (100 million yuan) | Increase over 2018(%) |
|---|---|---|---|---|
| Total | 40888 | -32.5 | 9415 | 5.8 |
| Of which: Agriculture, Forestry, Animal Husbandry and Fishery | 495 | -33.2 | 38 | -27.9 |
| Manufacturing | 5396 | -12.3 | 2416 | -11.0 |
| Production and Supply of Electricity, Heat Power, Gas and Water | 295 | 3.9 | 239 | -17.6 |
| Transport, Storage and Post | 591 | -21.6 | 309 | -1.6 |
| Information Transmission, Software and Information Technology | 4295 | -40.5 | 999 | 29.4 |
| Wholesale and Retail Trades | 13837 | -39.5 | 614 | -4.5 |
| Real Estate | 1050 | -0.3 | 1608 | 8.0 |
| Leasing and Business Services | 5777 | -36.5 | 1499 | 20.6 |
| Services to Households, Repair and Other Services | 361 | -25.6 | 37 | -0.4 |

In 2019, the non-financial outbound direct investment reached 763.0 billion yuan, down by 4.3 percent over that of the previous year, or 110.6 billion US dollars, down by 8.2 percent. Of this total, that to countries along the Belt and Road reached 15.0 billion US dollars, down by 3.8 percent.

### Table 14: Total Value of Non-financial Outbound Direct Investment and the Growth Rates in 2019

| Sector | Value (100 million US dollars) | Increase over 2018 (%) |
|---|---|---|
| Total | 1106.0 | -8.2 |
| Of which: Agriculture, Forestry, Animal Husbandry and Fishery | 15.4 | -13.0 |
| Mining | 75.2 | -18.5 |
| Manufacturing | 200.8 | 6.7 |
| Production and Supply of Electricity, Heat Power, Gas and Water | 25.2 | -20.5 |
| Construction | 85.1 | 15.6 |
| Wholesale and Retail Trades | 125.7 | 18.6 |
| Transport, Storage and Post | 55.5 | -4.3 |
| Information Transmission, Software and Information Technology | 61.2 | -10.5 |
| Real Estate | 48.2 | 22.0 |
| Leasing and Business Services | 355.6 | -20.3 |

In 2019, the accomplished business revenue through contracted overseas engineering projects was 1,192.8 billion yuan, up by 6.6 percent over that of the previous year, or 172.9 billion US dollars, up by 2.3 percent. Specifically, the accomplished business revenue from countries along the Belt and Road was 98.0 billion US dollars, an increase of 9.7 percent, accounting for 56.7 percent of the accomplished business revenue through contracted overseas engineering projects. The number of labor forces sent abroad through overseas labor contracts was 490 thousand.

VIII. Finance and Financial Intermediation

The national general public budget revenue reached 19,038.2 billion yuan in 2019, up by 3.8 percent over that of the previous year, of which tax revenue amounted to 15,799.2 billion yuan, an increase of 158.9 billion yuan, up by 1.0 percent. The national general public budget expenditure reached 23,887.4 billion yuan, up by 8.1 percent over that of the previous year.

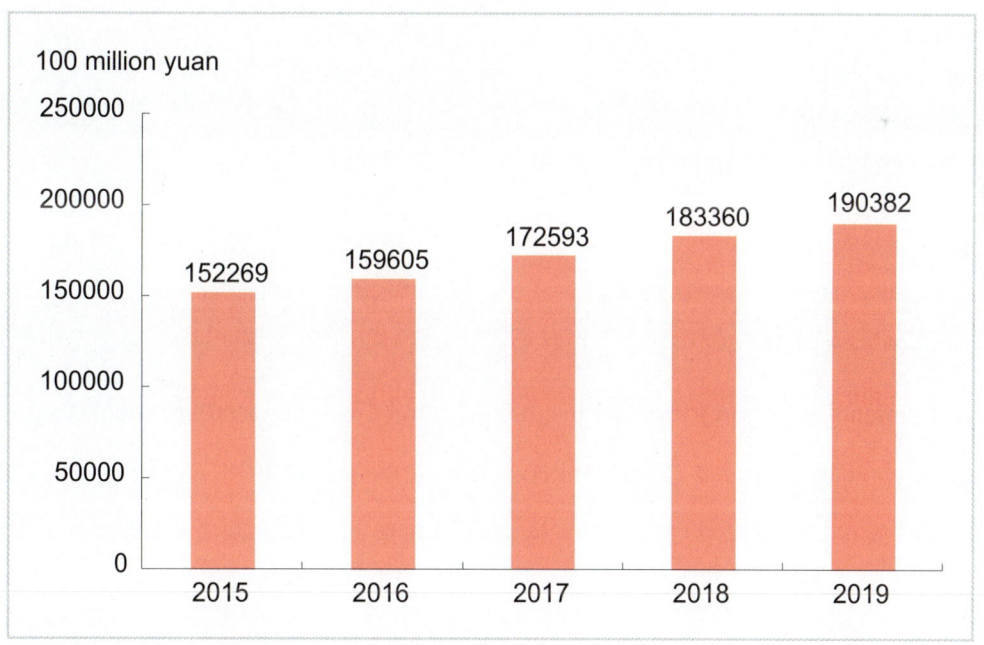

Figure 19: General Public Budget Revenue 2015-2019

Note: Data for general public budget revenue from 2015 to 2018 as shown in the figure were final accounts and that of 2019 was the executive accounts.

By the end of 2019, money supply of broad sense ($M_2$) was 198.6 trillion yuan, an increase of 8.7 percent over that by the end of the previous year. Money supply of narrow sense ($M_1$) was 57.6 trillion yuan, up by 4.4 percent. Cash in circulation ($M_0$) was 7.7 trillion yuan, up by 5.4 percent.

In 2019, the aggregate financing to the real economy (AFRE) (flow)[54] reached 25.6 trillion yuan, or 3.1 trillion yuan more than that in 2018 on a comparable basis. The AFRE (stock)[55] totaled 251.3 trillion yuan at the end of 2019, up by 10.7 percent over that at the end of 2018 on a comparable basis. Specifically, loans granted to the real economy in Renminbi stood at 151.6 trillion yuan, up by 12.5 percent. Savings deposit in Renminbi and foreign currencies in all items of financial institutions totaled 198.2 trillion yuan at the end of 2019, an increase of 15.7 trillion yuan compared with that at the beginning of the year. Of this total, the savings deposit in Renminbi stood at 192.9 trillion yuan, an increase of 15.4 trillion yuan. Loans in Renminbi and foreign currencies in all items of financial institutions reached 158.6 trillion yuan, an increase of 16.8 trillion yuan. Of this total, loans in Renminbi were 153.1 trillion yuan, an increase of 16.8 trillion yuan.

**Table 15: Savings Deposit and Loans in RMB and Foreign Currencies in All Financial Institutions and Growth Rates at the End of 2019**

| Item | Year-end figure (100 million yuan) | Increase over 2018 (%) |
| --- | --- | --- |
| **Savings deposit** | 1981643 | 8.6 |
| Domestic households | 821296 | 13.4 |
| Deposits in RMB | 813017 | 13.5 |
| Domestic non-financial enterprises | 621147 | 5.4 |
| **Loans** | 1586021 | 11.9 |
| Domestic short-term loans | 472380 | 6.6 |
| Domestic medium and long-term loans | 971805 | 13.7 |

Loans in Renminbi from rural financial institutions (rural credit cooperatives, rural cooperation banks and rural commercial banks) totaled 19,068.8 billion yuan by the end of 2019, an increase of 2,086.6 billion yuan as compared with that at the beginning of the year. Loans in Renminbi for consumption use from all financial institutions totaled 43,966.9 billion yuan, an increase of 6,166.7 billion yuan. Of the total, short-term personal loans totaled 9,922.6 billion yuan, an increase of 1,451.9 billion yuan, and medium and long-term personal loans reached 34,044.3 billion yuan, an increase of 4,714.8 billion yuan.

Funds raised through A-shares issued on Shanghai and Shenzhen Stock Exchanges[56] amounted to

---

54. The AFRE (flow) refers to the total volume of financing provided by the financial system to the real economy within a certain period of time. Adjustment was made to the statistical coverage of AFRE in 2019.
55. The AFRE (stock) refers to the outstanding financing provided by the financial system to the real economy at the end of a period of time (a month, a quarter or a year).
56. Funds raised through Shanghai and Shenzhen Stock Exchanges are calculated by the money raised on the listing date, and the funds raised include the actual exchanged convertible bonds, which were 8.0 billion yuan in 2018 and 99.5 billion yuan in 2019.

1,353.4 billion yuan in 2019, an increase of 207.6 billion yuan from the previous year. 201 A-shares were newly issued, raising 249.0 billion yuan worth of capital altogether, up by 111.2 billion yuan over that of the previous year. Of the total, 70 shares were from the science and technology innovation board, raising 82.4 billion yuan; refinancing of A-shares (including public newly issued, targeted placement, right issued, preferred stock and exchanged convertible bonds) raised 1,104.4 billion yuan, an increase of 96.4 billion yuan over that of the previous year. Various types of market entities financed 7,198.7 billion yuan through issuing bonds (including corporate bonds, convertible bonds, exchangeable bonds, financial bonds issued by policy banks, local government bonds and asset-backed securities) on Shanghai and Shenzhen Stock Exchanges, up by 1,510.9 billion yuan over that of the previous year. There were 8,953 companies listed on National Equities Exchange and Quotations[57] and funds raised by listed companies reached 26.5 billion yuan in 2019.

In 2019, 10.71 trillion yuan corporate debenture bonds[58] were issued, an increase of 2.92 trillion yuan over that of the previous year.

The premium of primary insurance received by the insurance companies[59] totaled 4,264.5 billion yuan in 2019, up by 12.2 percent over that of the previous year. Of this total, life insurance premium of primary insurance amounted to 2,275.4 billion yuan, health and casualty insurance premium of primary insurance 824.1 billion yuan, and property insurance premium of primary insurance 1,164.9 billion yuan. Insurance companies paid an indemnity worth of 1,289.4 billion yuan, of which, life insurance indemnity was 374.3 billion yuan, health and casualty insurance indemnity 264.9 billion yuan, and property insurance indemnity 650.2 billion yuan.

## IX. Households Income and Consumption and Social Security

In 2019, the per capita disposable income nationwide was 30,733 yuan, an increase of 8.9 percent over that of the previous year or a real increase of 5.8 percent after deducting price factors. The median[60] of per capita disposable income nationwide was 26,523 yuan, up by 9.0 percent. In terms of usual residence, the per capita disposable income of urban households was 42,359 yuan, up by 7.9 percent over that of 2018, or a

---

57. National Equities Exchange and Quotations, also called "the New Over-the-Counter Market", is a national securities exchange established upon approval by the State Council in 2012. Preferred stocks were excluded from funds raised by listed companies in National Equities Exchange and Quotations. Funds raised by shares are calculated by the disclosure date of the issuance report.
58. Corporate debenture bonds include debt financing instruments of non-financial businesses, enterprise bonds, corporate bonds and convertible bonds.
59. The premium of primary insurance received by the insurance companies refers to the premium income from primary insurance contracts confirmed by the insurance companies.
60. The median of per capita income refers to the per capita income of household lied in the middle of all surveyed households which are ranked from low to high (or high to low) based on per capita income level.

real growth of 5.0 percent after deducting price factors. The median of per capita disposable income of urban households was 39,244 yuan, up by 7.8 percent. The per capita disposable income of rural households was 16,021 yuan, up by 9.6 percent over that of the previous year, or 6.2 percent in real terms after deducting price factors. The median of per capita disposable income of rural households was 14,389 yuan, up by 10.1 percent. Grouped by income quintile[61], the per capita disposable income of low-income group reached 7,380 yuan, the lower-middle-income group 15,777 yuan, the middle-income group 25,035 yuan, the upper-middle-income group 39,230 yuan and the high-income group 76,401 yuan. The per capita monthly income of migrant workers was 3,962 yuan, increased by 6.5 percent over that of the previous year.

The national per capita consumption expenditure was 21,559 yuan, up by 8.6 percent over that of the previous year, or a real growth of 5.5 percent after deducting price factors. Specifically, the per capita consumption expenditure on services[62] totaled 9,886 yuan, up by 12.6 percent over that of the previous year, accounting for 45.9 percent of the per capita consumption expenditure. In terms of usual residence, the per capita consumption expenditure of urban households was 28,063 yuan, up by 7.5 percent, or 4.6 percent in real terms after deducting price factors. The per capita consumption expenditure of rural households was 13,328 yuan, up by 9.9 percent, or a real growth of 6.5 percent after deducting price factors. The national Engel's Coefficient stood at 28.2 percent, 0.2 percentage point lower than that of the previous year, with that of urban and rural households standing at 27.6 percent and 30.0 percent respectively.

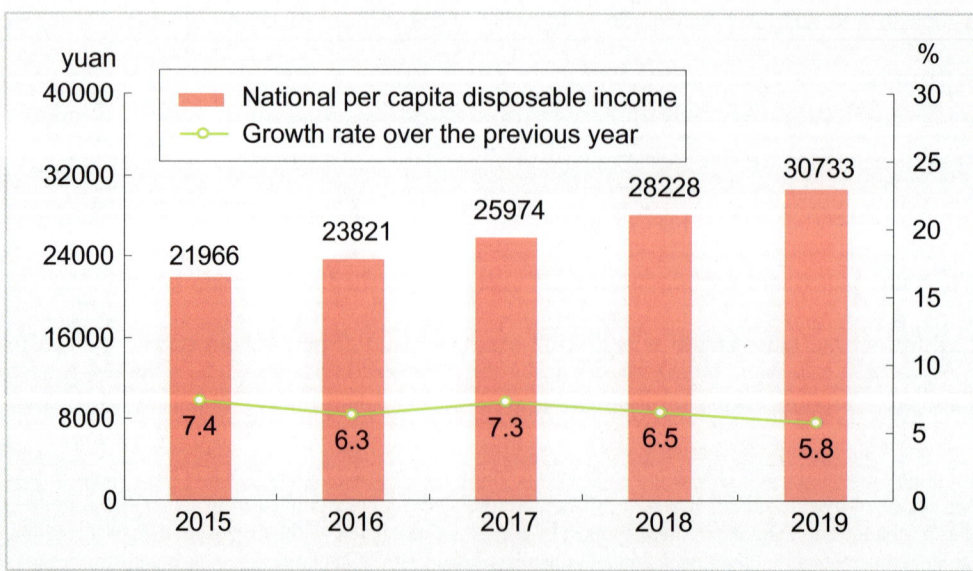

Figure 20: National Per Capita Disposable Income and its Growth Rates 2015-2019

---

61. The income quintile refers to the five equal partitions of all surveyed households, who are ranked from low to high based on per capita income level. The top 20 percent with the highest income are classified as high-income group, and the other four levels are upper-middle-income group, middle-income group, lower-middle-income group and low-income group.

62. The consumption expenditure on services refers to the spending by surveyed households on non-commodity services for daily lives.

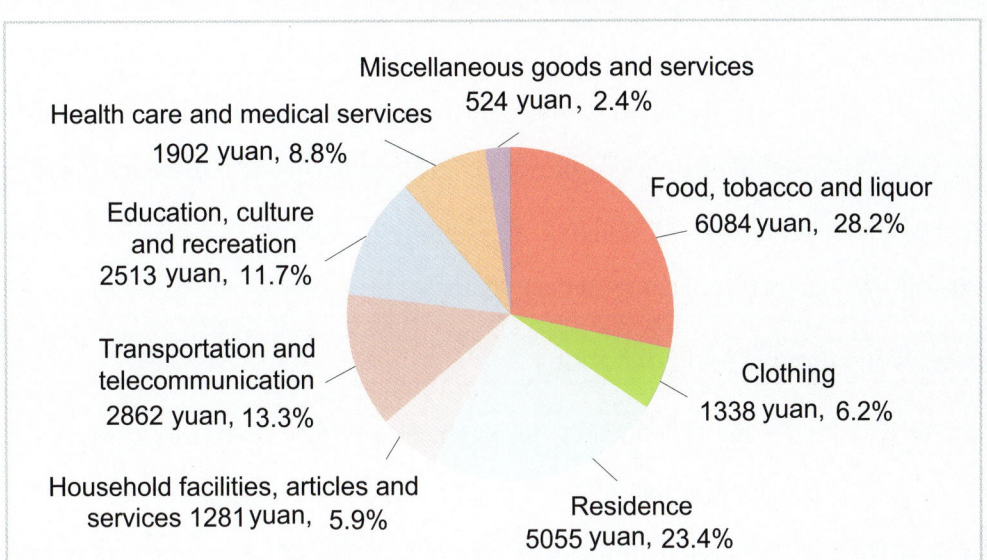

**Figure 21: National Per Capita Consumption Expenditure and Composition in 2019**

By the end of 2019, a total of 434.82 million people participated in basic endowment insurance program for urban workers, an increase of 15.81 million over that by the end of 2018. A total of 532.66 million people participated in basic endowment insurance program for urban and rural residents, an increase of 8.74 million. A total of 1,354.36 million people participated in basic medical insurance program, an increase of 9.78 million. Of this total, 329.26 million people participated in the program for workers, an increase of 12.45 million, and 1,025.10 million people participated in the program for urban and rural residents. Some 205.43 million people participated in unemployment insurance program, an increase of 8.99 million. The number of people receiving unemployment insurance payment stood at 2.28 million by the end of 2019. A total of 254.74 million people participated in work-related injury insurance, an increase of 16.00 million, of which 86.16 million were migrant workers, an increase of 5.30 million. A total of 214.32 million people participated in maternity insurance programs, an increase of 9.97 million. Minimum living allowances were granted to 8.61 million urban residents and 34.56 million rural residents, and 4.39 million rural residents living in extreme poverty[63] received relief and assistance and 9.18 million people received temporary assistance[64]. A total of 77.82 million people were financed to participate in basic medical insurance program and outpatient

---

63. Rural residents living in extreme poverty refer to the aged, the disabled and the minor under 16 years of age in rural areas who have no ability to work, no sources of income and no statutory obligors to provide for them, bring them up or support them, or whose statutory obligors have no ability to fulfill their obligations.

64. Temporary assistance refers to emergent and transitional assistance the government provides to families or individuals who experience hardships because of emergencies, unexpected harm, major diseases or other unusual factors and are not covered by other forms of social assistance programs or still suffer hardships after receiving other social assistance programs.

and inpatient assistance were granted to 61.80 million recipients. National subsidies and allowances were provided to 8.61 million veterans and other entitled people in 2019.

By the end of 2019, there were altogether 37 thousand social welfare institutions providing accommodation, of which 34 thousand were elderly caring organizations and 663 were children caring organizations. The social welfare institutions provided 7.901 million beds[65], of which 7.614 million were for the elderly and 97 thousand were for children. By the end of 2019, there were 26 thousand community service centers and 167 thousand community service stations.

## X. Science & Technology and Education

Expenditures on research and experimental development activities (R&D) were worth 2,173.7 billion yuan in 2019, up by 10.5 percent over that of 2018, accounting for 2.19 percent of GDP. Of this total, 120.9 billion yuan was used for basic research programs. A total of 234 subject researches were arranged under the national science and technology major projects and 45,192 projects were financed by the National Natural Science Foundation. By the end of 2019, there were altogether 515 state key laboratories in operation, 133 national engineering research centers, 217 national engineering laboratories, and 1,540 state-level enterprise technology centers. The National Fund for Technology Transfer and Commercialization established 21 sub-funds, with the total size reaching 31.3 billion yuan. There were 1,177 state-level technology business incubators[66] and 1,888 national mass makerspaces[67]. There were 4,380 thousand patent applications from home and abroad, up by 1.3 percent over that of the previous year, and a total of 2,592 thousand were authorized, up by 5.9 percent. The number of PCT patent applications accepted[68] was 61 thousand. By the end of 2019, the number of patents in force was 9,722 thousand, of which 1,862 thousand were invention patents from home. The number of invention patents per 10,000 people was 13.3. Trademark application reached 7,837 thousand, up by 6.3 percent over that of the previous year; trademark registration totaled 6,406

---

65. The beds provided by social welfare institutions include beds provided by adoption agencies, aid agencies and community agencies.
66. The state-level technology business incubators are technology-based business startup service providers consistent with the *Administrative Measures for Technology Business Incubators* that provide physical space, shared facilities and professional services with the mission of advancing transformation of technological achievements, cultivating technological enterprises and fostering the entreprenuerial spirit. They should be approved and accredited by the Ministry of Science and Technology.
67. The national mass makerspaces are new service platform for entrepreneurship and innovation that are in comformity with the Guidelines on Developing Mass Makerspaces and are reviewed and registered by Torch High Technology Industry Development Center of the Ministry of Science and Technology in accordance with the *Provisional Registration Regulations on National Mass Makerspaces*.
68. The number of PCT patent applications accepted refers to the number of PCT patent application accepted by the State Intellectual Property Office which acts as the receiving office of PCT patent application. PCT is the abbreviation of Patent Cooperation Treaty, which is a treaty for international cooperation in the field of patents.

thousand, up by 27.9 percent over that of the previous year. A total of 484 thousand technology transfer contracts were signed, representing 2,239.8 billion yuan in value, up by 26.6 percent over that of the previous year.

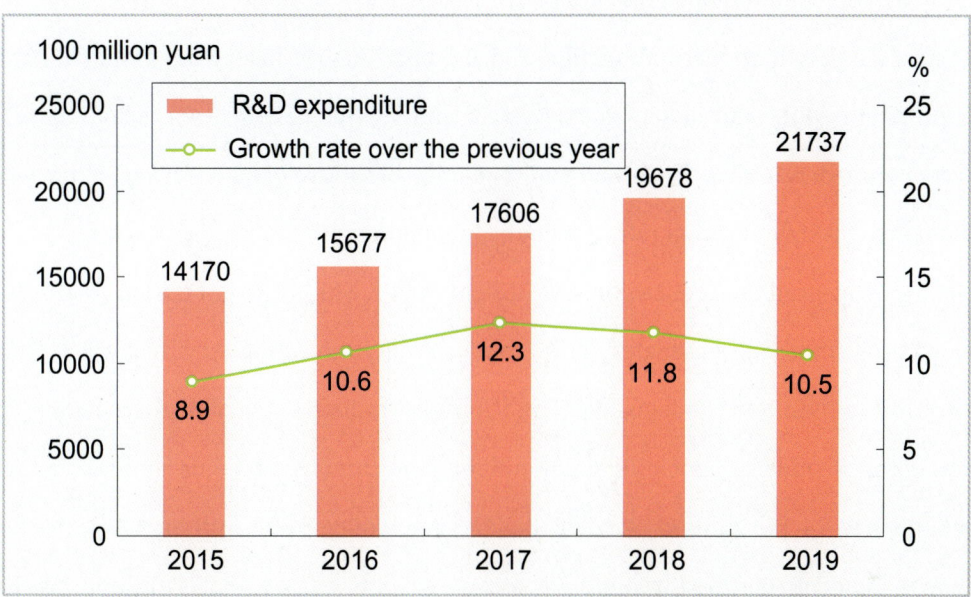

Figure 22: The Amount of Expenditure on Research and Experimental Development Activities (R&D) and its Growth Rates 2015-2019

Table 16: Number of Patent Applications, Patents Authorized and Patents in Force in 2019

| Item | Patents (10,000) | Increase over 2018 (%) |
| --- | --- | --- |
| **Number of patent applications** | 438.0 | 1.3 |
| Of which: domestic | 417.2 | 1.2 |
| Of which: for new inventions | 140.1 | -9.2 |
| Of which: domestic | 123.1 | -10.8 |
| **Number of patents authorized** | 259.2 | 5.9 |
| Of which: domestic | 245.8 | 6.0 |
| Of which: for new inventions | 45.3 | 4.8 |
| Of which: domestic | 35.4 | 4.3 |
| **Number of patents in force at the end of the year** | 972.2 | 16.0 |
| Of which: domestic | 869.2 | 17.5 |
| Of which: for new inventions | 267.1 | 12.9 |
| Of which: domestic | 186.2 | 16.3 |

The year 2019 saw 32 times of successful satellite launches. Carrier rocket the Long March-5 Y3 and Gaofen-7 satellite were successfully launched. The Long March carrier rocket series completed its 300 launches. Chang´e-4 probe made the first-ever soft landing and exploration on the far side of the moon. The solid-propellant carrier rocket was successfully launched at sea. The deployment of the core constellation of Beidou-3 global system was completed. Xuelong 2 made its maiden voyage to the Antarctic. The first home-built aircraft carrier was commissioned into active service.

By the end of 2019, there were altogether 835 national quality inspection centers. There were 596 agencies for product quality and management system and service certification, accumulatively 720,000 enterprises were certified. A total of 2,021 national standards were developed or revised in the year, including 1,448 new standards. The qualification rate of manufactured products[69] reached 93.86 percent.

In 2019, the post-graduate education enrollment was 2.864 million students with 917 thousand new students and 640 thousand graduates. The general tertiary education enrollment was 30.315 million students with 9.149 million new students and 7.585 million graduates. Vocational secondary schools[70] had 15.765 million enrolled students, including 6.004 million new entrants, and 4.934 million graduates. Senior secondary schools had 24.143 million enrolled students, including 8.395 million new entrants, and 7.892 million graduates. Students enrolled in junior secondary schools totaled 48.271 million, including 16.388 million new entrants, and 14.541 million graduates. The country had a primary education enrollment of 105.612 million students, including 18.690 million new entrants, and 16.479 million graduates. There were 795 thousand students enrolled in special education schools, with 144 thousand new entrants and 98 thousand graduates. Kindergartens accommodated 47.139 million children. The number of students graduating from compulsory education reached 94.8 percent of the total enrollment, and the gross enrollment ratio for senior secondary education reached 89.5 percent.

---

69. The qualification rate of manufactured products is the ratio of the samples that have passed the sampling quality test, the process of which follows certain methods, procedure and standard, to the total amount of the sampled products. The survey samples cover 29 sectors of the manufacturing industry.

70. Vocational secondary schools include regular specialized secondary schools, adult specialized secondary schools, vocational high schools and skilled workers schools.

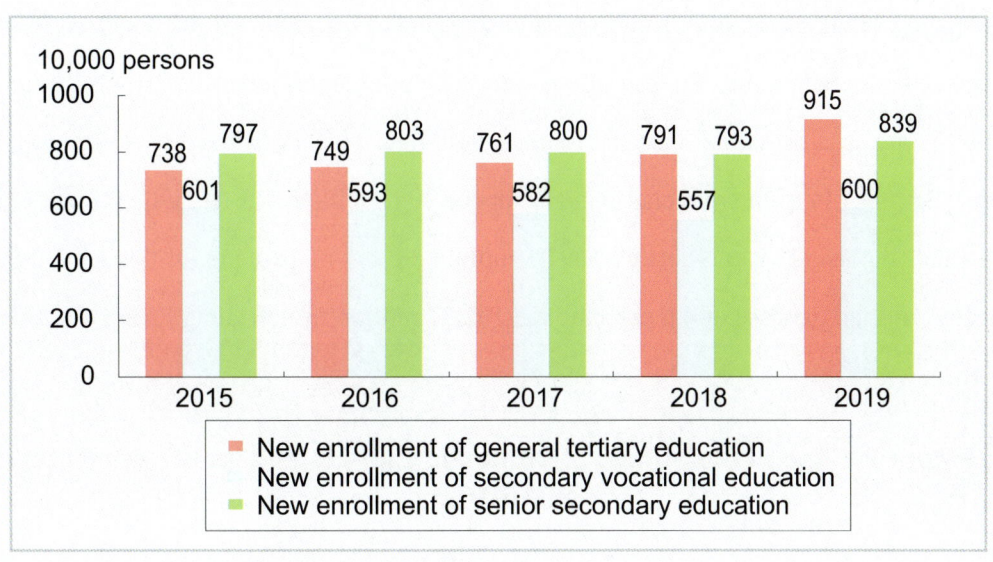

**Figure 23: Enrollment in Education 2015-2019**

## XI. Culture and Tourism, Public Health and Sports

By the end of 2019, there were 2,072 art-performing groups and 3,410 museums in the culture and tourism system throughout China. A total of 3,189 public libraries received[71] 877.74 million people. There were 3,325 cultural centers. Subscribers to cable television programs numbered 212 million, in which 198 million subscribed to digital cable television programs. By the end of 2019, radio broadcasting and television broadcasting coverage rates were 99.1 percent and 99.4 percent respectively. A total of 10,646 episodes of 254 TV series and 94,659 minutes of TV cartoons were made in 2019. The country produced 850 feature movies and 187 popular science movies, documentaries, animation and special movies[72]. A total of 31.5 billion copies of newspapers and 2.2 billion copies of magazines were issued, and 10.2 billion copies of books were published. The average number of books possessed per person[73] was 7.29 copies. By the end of the year, there were 4,136 archives in China and 143.41 million files were made accessible to the public. The business revenue of enterprises above the designated size engaged in culture and related industries reached 8,662.4 billion yuan, up by 7.0 percent over that of the previous year on a comparable basis.

The year 2019 registered 6.01 billion domestic tourists, up by 8.4 percent over that of the previous

---

71. The people received by the public libraries refer to the number of people who visit libraries and use library services in the year, including borrowing and reading books, consultation and attending readers' programs.
72. Special movies refer to those using different display modes in terms of projection techniques, equipment and program as compared with the ordinary cinemas, such as IMAX movies, 3D movies, 4D movies, multidimensional movies and full dome movies.
73. The average number of books possessed per person refers to the average number of books published in the year that can be possessed per person in China.

year. The revenue from domestic tourism totaled 5,725.1 billion yuan, up by 11.7 percent. The number of inbound visitors to China totaled 145.31 million, an increase of 2.9 percent. Of this total, 31.88 million were foreigners, up by 4.4 percent; and 113.42 million were Chinese compatriots from Hong Kong, Macao and Taiwan, up by 2.5 percent. Of all the inbound tourists, overnight visitors counted 65.73 million, an increase of 4.5 percent. Earnings from international tourism topped 131.3 billion US dollars, up by 3.3 percent. The number of China's outbound visitors totaled 169.21 million, up by 4.5 percent. Of this total, 162.11 million were on private visits, an increase of 4.6 percent; and 102.37 million visited Hong Kong, Macao and Taiwan, up by 3.2 percent.

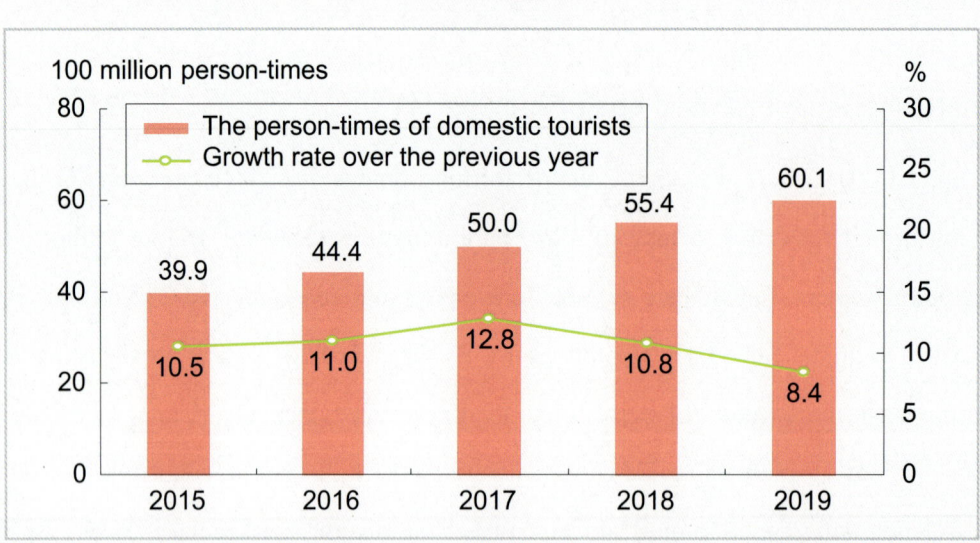

Figure 24: The Person-times of Domestic Tourists and its Growth Rates 2015-2019

By the end of 2019, there were 1,014,000 medical and health institutions in China, including 34,000 hospitals. Of all the hospitals, 12,000 were public, and 22,000 were private. Of the 960,000 medical and health institutions at grass-root level, there were 36,000 town and township health centers, 35,000 community health service centers, 267,000 clinics and 621,000 village clinics. Of the 17,000 professional public health institutions, 3,456 were disease control and prevention centers and 3,106 were health monitoring institutions. By the end of 2019, there were 10.10 million medical technical personnel in China, including 3.82 million licensed doctors and licensed assistant doctors and 4.43 million registered nurses. The medical and health institutions in China possessed 8.92 million beds, of which, hospitals possessed 6.97 million and township health centers had 1.38 million. The total number of medical visits[74] and hospital discharges[75] in 2019 reached 8.52 billion and 270 million respectively.

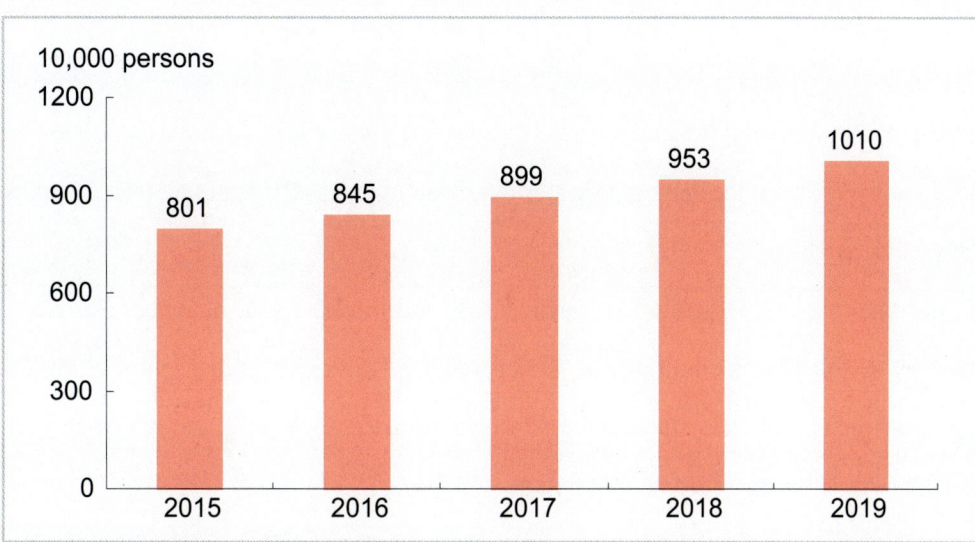

Figure 25: Year-end Number of Medical Technical Personnel 2015-2019

There were altogether 3.162 million sports venues[76]. The sports venue area[77] totaled 2.59 billion square meters and the per capita sports venue area reached 1.86 square meters. In 2019, Chinese athletes won 128 world championships in 33 sports events and broke 16 world records. Chinese physically-challenged athletes won 350 world championships in 53 international sports competitions.

XII. Resources, Environment and Emergency Management

In 2019, the total supply of state-owned land for construction use[78] was 624 thousand hectares, a decrease of 3.6 percent over that of the previous year. Of this total, the supply for mining storage was 147 thousand hectares, up by 10.3 percent; that for real estate[79] was 142 thousand hectares, down by 1.4 percent; and that for infrastructure facilities was 335 thousand hectares, down by 9.5 percent.

---

74. The total number of medical visits refers to the number of people receiving medical services, including outpatient services, emergency treatment, home visits, appointment-based diagnosis and treatment, health check-up of a specific item, and health consultation and guidance (excluding health lectures).

75. The number of hospital discharges refers to the number of inpatients discharged from hospitals in the reporting period, including those who are discharged from hospitals or transferred to other medical institutions following doctors' advice, discharged from hospitals without doctors' permission, dead or other situations. The number of people who are recovered from family sickbeds is excluded.

76. Data on sports venues are from the results of the seventh natinal census on sports venues. The sports venues belonging to armed forces and railway system are excluded in the census on sports venues. Data is as of the end of 2018.

77. The sports venue area refers to area used for physical training, sports competitions and physical fitness.

78. Total supply of state-owned land for construction use refers to the total amount of state-owned land for construction use with the land-use right transferred, allocated or leased to units or individuals through signed transaction contracts and allocation decisions by the municipal or county governments according to annual land supply plan and in line with relevant laws in the reporting period.

79. Land used for real estate refers to the sum of land used for commercial service and for residence.

The total stock of water resources in 2019 was 2,867.0 billion cubic meters. With a decrease of 0.4 percent over 2018, the total water consumption reached 599.1 billion cubic meters, of which water consumption for living purposes up by 1.9 percent, for industrial use down by 2.1 percent, for agricultural use down by 0.5 percent, and for ecological water supplement grew by 0.5 percent. Water consumption for every 10 thousand yuan worth of GDP produced[80] was 67 cubic meters, a decline of 6.1 percent over that of the previous year. Water consumption for every 10 thousand yuan worth of industrial value added was 42 cubic meters, down by 7.2 percent. Per capita water consumption was 429 cubic meters, down by 0.8 percent over that of the previous year.

In 2019, the total area of afforestation reached 7.07 million hectares, of which 3.65 million hectares were afforested by manpower, accounting for 51.6 percent of the total. Forest tending areas reached 7.73 million hectares. By the end of 2019, there were 474 national natural reserves. A total of 54 thousand square kilometers of land have been saved from soil erosion.

Preliminary estimation indicated that the total energy consumption[81] in 2019 amounted to 4.86 billion tons of standard coal equivalent, up by 3.3 percent over that of 2018. The consumption of coal increased by 1.0 percent; crude oil, up by 6.8 percent; natural gas, up by 8.6 percent; and electric power, up by 4.5 percent. The consumption of coal accounted for 57.7 percent of the total energy consumption, 1.5 percentage points lower than that of 2018, while clean energy consumption, such as natural gas, hydropower, nuclear power and wind power accounted for 23.4 percent, 1.3 percentage points higher. The comprehensive energy consumption per unit calcium carbide by key energy-intensive industrial enterprises went down by 2.1 percent, per unit synthetic ammonia down by 2.4 percent, per ton steel down by 1.3 percent and per unit electrolytic aluminium down by 2.2 percent. The standard coal consumption per kilowatt-hour of thermal power generation decreased by 0.3 percent. The carbon dioxide emission per 10,000 yuan worth of GDP was cut by 4.1 percent.

---

80. The consumption of water for producing 10 thousand yuan worth of GDP and 10 thousand yuan worth of industrial value added are calculated at 2015 constant prices.

81. Historical data of the total energy consumption and related indicators were revised according to the results of the Fourth National Economic Census.

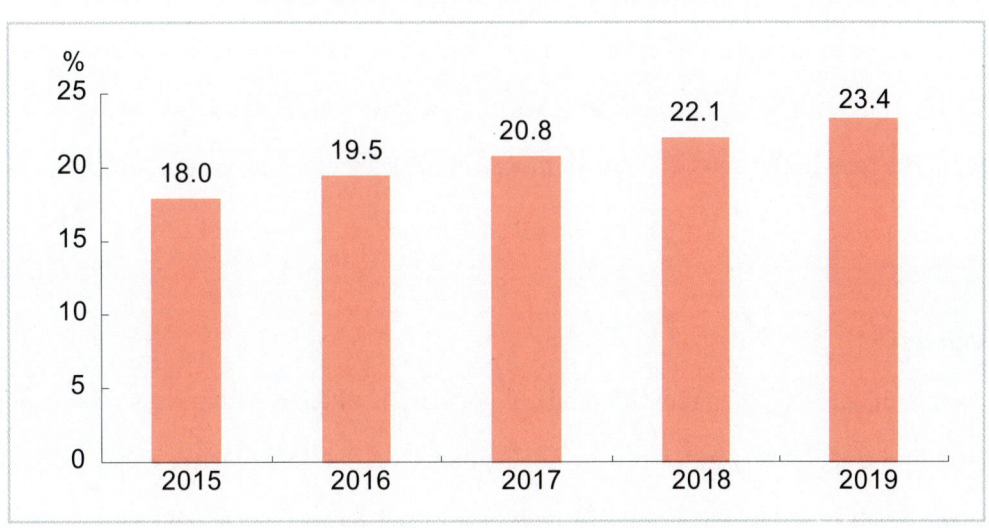

**Figure 26: The Proportion of Clean Energy Consumption in the Total Energy Consumption 2015-2019**

Monitoring of oceanic water quality at 1,257 offshore monitoring stations indicated that oceanic water met the national quality standard Grade I and II at 76.6 percent of the stations; water quality at 7.0 percent of the stations met Grade III standard; and water of Grade IV or inferior quality was found at 16.4 percent of the stations.

Of the monitored 337 cities at prefecture level and above, 46.6 percent reached the air standard and 53.4 percent failed. The annual average concentration of particulate matter ($PM_{2.5}$) for cities that failed to meet the standard (cities failed to meet the standard of annual average $PM_{2.5}$ concentration in 2015) stood at 40 micrograms per cubic meter, down by 2.4 percent over that of the previous year.

Of the 322 cities subject to noise monitoring program, 2.5 percent enjoyed fairly good environment, 66.8 percent had good environment, 28.9 percent had fair environment, 1.9 percent had poor environment in downtown areas.

The average temperature in 2019 was 10.34℃, up by 0.25℃ compared with that of the previous year. Typhoons hit China 5 times in 2019.

In 2019, natural disasters hit 19.26 million hectares of crops, of which 2.80 million hectares of crops were demolished. Flood, waterlogging and geological disasters caused a direct economic loss of 192.3 billion yuan. Droughts caused a direct economic loss of 45.7 billion yuan. Disasters caused by low temperature, frost and snow made a total direct economic loss of 2.8 billion yuan. Oceanic disasters caused a direct economic loss of 11.7 billion yuan. The country recorded 20 earthquakes with magnitude 5.0 and over, 13 of which caused disasters, causing a direct economic loss of 5.9 billion yuan. The year 2019 witnessed 2,345 forest fires, with 14 thousand hectares of forests damaged.

The death toll due to work accidents amounted to 29,519 people. Work accidents in industrial, mining and commercial companies caused 1.474 deaths out of every 100 thousand employees, down by 4.7 percent over that of 2018. The death toll for one million tons of coal produced in coalmines was 0.083 people, down by 10.8 percent. The road traffic death toll per 10 thousand vehicles was 1.80 people, down by 6.7 percent.

**Data Sources:**

In this Communiqué, data of urbanization rate of population with household registration, motor vehicles for civilian use and traffic accidents are from the Ministry of Public Security; data of newly increased employed people in urban areas, registered unemployment rate, social security and skilled workers schools are from the Ministry of Human Resources and Social Security; data of foreign exchange reserves and exchange rates are from the State Administration of Foreign Exchange; data of market entities, quality inspection, the formulation and revision of national standards and qualification rate of manufactured products are from the State Administration for Market Regulation; data of cutting taxes and fees are from the State Taxation Administration; data of output of aquatic products and area of farmland newly equipped with effective water-saving irrigation systems are from the Ministry of Agriculture and Rural Affairs; data of production of timber, area of afforestation, forest tending areas and national natural reserves are from the National Forestry and Grassland Administration; data of area of farmland newly equipped with irrigation system, water resources and land newly saved from soil erosion are from the Ministry of Water Resources; data of installed power generation capacity, newly increased power transformer equipment with a capacity of 220 kilovolts and above and electricity consumption are from the China Electricity Council; data of volume of freight handled by ports, container shipping of ports, highway transportation, waterway transportation, new and rebuilt highways and new throughput capacity of berths for over 10,000-tonnage ships are from the Ministry of Transport; data of railway transportation, new railways put into operation, new double-track railways put into operation and electrified railways put into operation are from China Railway; data of civil aviation and new civil transportation airports are from the Civil Aviation Administration of China; data of pipelines are from China National Petroleum Corporation, China Petrochemical Corporation and China National Offshore Oil Corporation; data of postal service are from State Post Bureau; data of telecommunication, software revenue, and new lines of optical-fiber cables are from the Ministry of Industry and Information Technology; data of housing units rebuilt or renovated in rundown urban areas and for poverty-stricken rural households with economic status registered at the local governments are from the Ministry of Housing and Urban-Rural Development; data of imports and exports of goods are from the General Administration of Customs; data of imports and exports of services, foreign direct investment, outbound direct investment, overseas contracted projects and overseas labor contracts are from the Ministry of Commerce; data of finance are from the Ministry of Finance; data of monetary finance and corporate debenture bonds are from the People's Bank of China; data of funds raised through domestic exchange markets are from China Securities Regulatory Commission; data of the insurance sector are from China Banking and Insurance Regulatory Commission; data of medical insurance, maternity insurance, people financed to participate in basic medical insurance program, and outpatient and inpatient assistance recipients are from the National Healthcare and Security Administration; data of urban and rural minimum living allowances, relief and assistance granted to rural residents living in extreme poverty, temporary assistance and social services are from the Ministry of Civil Affairs; data of entitled people are from the Ministry of Veterans Affairs; data of national science and technology major projects, state key laboratories, National Fund for Technology Transfer and Commercialization, state-level technology business incubators, national mass makerspaces and technology transfer contracts are from the Ministry of Science and Technology; data of natural science foundation projects are from the National Natural Science Foundation; data of national engineering research centers, national engineering laboratories and enterprise technical centers are from the National Development and Reform Commission; data of patents and trademarks are from the National Intellectual Property Administration; data of satellite launches are from the State Administration of Science, Technology and Industry for National Defense; data of education are from the Ministry of Education; data of art-performing groups, museums, public libraries, cultural centers, books and tourism are from the Ministry of Culture and Tourism; data of television and radio programs are from the National Radio and Television Administration; data of movies are from the China Film Administration; data of newspapers and magazines are from the National Press and Publication Administration; data of files are from the State Archives Administration; data of outbound visitors are from the National Immigration Administration; data of medical care and health are from the National Health Commission; data of sports are from the General Administration of Sport; data of physically-challenged athletes are from the China Disabled Persons' Federation; data of supply of state-owned land for construction use and direct economic loss caused by oceanic disasters are from the Ministry of Natural Resources; data of the carbon dioxide emission per 10,000 yuan worth of GDP and environment monitoring are from the Ministry of Ecology and Environment; data of average temperature and typhoons are from the China Meteorological Administration; data of areas of crops hit by natural disasters, direct economic loss caused by flood, waterlogging and geological disasters, direct economic loss caused by droughts, direct economic loss caused by low temperature, frost and snow, forest fires, areas of forests damaged and work safety are from the Ministry of Emergency Management; data of the number of earthquakes and direct economic loss caused by earthquakes are from the China Earthquake Administration; all the other data are from the National Bureau of Statistics.

---

In case of any differences between English translation and the original Chinese text, the Chinese edition shall prevail.